Alic

Check Out

For Nick and Louis

Check it Out

Published as a Mandarin paperback by Mitchell Beazley,
an imprint of Reed Consumer Books Ltd,
Michelin House, 81 Fulham Road, London SW3 6RB
and Auckland, Melbourne, Singapore and Toronto

Reprinted 1994 (twice)

A CIP catalogue record for this book is available from the British Library.

ISBN 0 7493 1841 4

Executive Editor: Anne Ryland
Editor: Susan Keevil
Art Editor: Paul Tilby
Indexer: Angie Hipkin
Production: Michelle Thomas

Printed and bound in Great Britain by
Cox & Wyman Ltd, Reading, Berkshire
Typeset in Baskerville
Jacket photographs:
James Johnson (front)
Robin MacLeod (back)

CONTENTS

INTRODUCTION

There has never been such a good time to buy wine. Today, the choice costing under a fiver is staggering. There are wines from nearly every part of the globe and made from all kinds of grape varieties. And not only is the range much better than it has ever been, but the general quality is becoming more and more impressive.

Why, you may ask, do the supermarkets offer such a huge range in this price bracket? The simple answer is that wines at under £5 a bottle account for around 90 percent of their sales in volume terms.

Check it Out selects the best of these wines, describing what they taste like, which dishes go best with them, and, most importantly, where to buy them. Any wine found in *Check it Out* is there only because it is good enough to recommend.

How the wines were selected for *Check it Out*

I asked each supermarket to preselect what they thought to be their best wines under a fiver and submit them for tasting. In addition, they had to adhere to two criteria:

1. The wines had to be available from 80 percent of their stores.

2. The wines had to come from suppliers they dealt with or intended to deal with on a regular, long term basis. This was to try to avoid recommending wines only stocked for a short time.

Every effort has been made to ensure *Check it Out* is as up-to-date as possible. Many of the supermarkets helped by providing advance samples of wines not in the stores at the time of writing, but which will now be on the shelves. If a given vintage has changed, be daring and try the new one.

How the tasting was done

All the wines for possible inclusion in *Check it Out* were tasted over an intensive six week period. Only the best wines were selected, and hundreds that did not come up to scratch were excluded.

The wine tastings were carried out by style, like with like from each of the stores. For example, dry whites of the same or similar character (eg Muscadets) were tasted and compared with each other, and so on. *Check it Out* is the only supermarket guide to have conducted its tastings in this way. The other guides taste wines in supermarket order only, and not comparatively.

This means that if a wine is recommended in *Check it Out*, it is one of the best of its kind available, rather than just the best wine a certain store has of a given type. For example, if one supermarket's Muscadet did not do well in the comparative tasting, then no Muscadet will be listed for it in *Check it Out*.

The quality of the wines in the tastings was exceptionally high, proof that the supermarkets rightly pay a great deal of attention to the quality of their wines under £5. And, whilst I intended to include around five hundred wines, the quality was so good that I have had to recommend nearly six hundred. You will not be disappointed by any of them.

How to use *Check it Out*

It's easy.

Look up the supermarket you are planning to visit. Then decide on the style of wine you are looking for: red or white, light or full-bodied, dry or sweet, and so on. You'll find the wines divided into these categories in the book, rather than countries, which means you can see at a glance what a choice you have from across the world.

Within each style section, the wines are arranged alphabetically, and the wine's name is shown in the same order throughout the book, that's to say: grape variety (if any), area, producer. This makes it easier to compare similar wines, and experiment with new ones. So if, for instance, you favour Chardonnay, you will be able to see at a glance which Chardonnays a particular supermarket stocks.

If you are after a specific wine, look it up in the index and check which supermarkets stock it. If you find an old favourite, it's a good idea to experiment with another wine in the same section, as it may well be very similar.

Take *Check it Out* with you when shopping, so that you can look up wines as you find them on the shelf.

The secret to enjoying bargain wine buys is being prepared to try out new ones: during the tastings for this book, the most disappointing were normally those with well known names, like Muscadet, Soave, Côtes du Rhône, Chianti and so on, whereas the best wines are often those with more unfamiliar names.

But if you are merely looking for one wine in any of the supermarkets listed here, you cannot go wrong with one of the Star Buys chosen as the best value and most interesting red and white the supermarket has to offer. Happy drinking!

Vintages and prices

Whilst every care has been taken to ensure that the vintages and prices of wines detailed in *Check it Out* are the same as those on sale, it is possible that some will have changed. If a more recent vintage is in stock, the quality should be comparable, and therefore a similar buy. (With the majority of whites, especially light and medium-dry whites, a rule of thumb is 'the younger the vintage, the fresher the wine'.)

Essential equipment – an acknowledgement

The only corkscrew up to the challenge of opening the many wines tasted for *Check it Out* was the trusty Screwpull. While I used the industrial-quality Lever Screwpull, I can equally vouch for the standard and pocket-size varieties. They make opening a bottle of wine a pleasure rather than a chore.

A guide to the wine styles in *Check it Out*

Light Dry Whites

If it's dry white you are after, the choice is mind-bogglingly massive.

Light dry whites account for more wines than any other style in this book, with contenders from all around the globe. Just about every country imaginable produces wines in this category.

Ten years ago, it was one of the least reliable wine styles around. But huge advances in technology have lead to dramatic improvements, which is great news for us, the consumers. Now, grapes are picked before they become overripe, and as a result maintain their crisp, tangy, fruity acidity. Cold fermentation then ensures this zippy fruit is locked into the wine, and better hygiene in the winery means that fewer wines become tainted by bacteria.

One of the biggest disappointments of the *Check it Out* tastings was the quality of one of Britain's biggest-selling dry white wines, Muscadet. Many were thin and insipid. And Burgundy, the world's most famous quality white producing region, hardly fared any better. Other lesser known areas of France, however, are now producing impressive wines, especially Chardonnays from the south.

The wines of Bulgaria were more consistent than Muscadet, and also excellent value for money. Hungary is a relative newcomer to the modern winemaking scene, but it is already revealing spectacular results.

South Africa deserves a special mention as the quality of its wines proved to be particularly good, especially the Chardonnays, Sauvignons and the floral Colombards. If you've yet to try one, now is the ideal time.

Many people think of German wines as medium-dry only, yet there are dry wines, especially from areas like the (relatively) sunny Baden, well worth trying.

In Italy, as in France, the most well known wines, Soave and Frascati, yielded the most disappointments. Instead, be more adventurous and try Bianco di Custoza, Pinot Grigio or an Italian Chardonnay.

Australia, not surprisingly, came up trumps with many easy-drinking, tasty, well priced dry wines, which were of a consistently high quality. And even good old England had a few impressive ones to offer.

So the message with dry white is don't stick to the old favourites. You'll get much better value for money and make many more exciting finds by looking further afield.

Light dry whites are perfect aperitif wines, and can be drunk at any time of the day or night. They are ideal to have in store for when unexpected guests drop in – always keep a couple of bottles in the fridge. They also complement a whole host of similarly light dishes, like soup, pasta, salads, seafood, white fish, white meat and certain mild cheeses.

Medium-Dry Whites

Quality medium-dry wines have a flavour of grapey sweetness but also an attractive touch of acidity, a citrusy tang on the aftertaste.

Most wines in this style are from Germany, and the quality is exceptionally high. Unlike France and Italy, where the best selling wines were often of the poorest quality, Germany produced some tasty popular surprises. There are several Liebfraumilchs, Niersteiners and Piesporters recommended in this book which will not disappoint. (If you want to move on to German wines with more complexity look for wines made entirely from the Riesling grape.)

In France the most interesting wines are Vouvrays, made from the honeyed Chenin Blanc grape grown in the Loire Valley. It's also successful in Australia and South Africa where it produces equally tasty results.

Medium-dry whites are great party wines, easy to drink on their own and guaranteed to please those who don't favour bone dry styles. While they make good aperitifs, they also go well with all kinds of food. The sweetness and the acidity mean they complement two different type of dishes: you can either drink them with soup, fish pâté, white fish, spicy seafood like prawns in garlic, scallops, chicken, guinea-fowl, turkey or any meat (like duck) served in a fruit sauce; or they go equally well with fruit salad, fruit crumble, fruit tarts, and medium strength cheeses.

Full-Bodied Dry Whites

Dry, yet rich in fruit, many of the wines in this category have been aged in oak. This gives them an added complexity, with nuances of toasted oak and vanilla, and adds a general roundness and weightiness.

Some of the world's most expensive whites, like white burgundy star Puligny-Montrachet, would be in this style group, though sadly they are never under a fiver – and nor are many wines from Burgundy. But the good news is that quite a few wines made from the same grape – Chardonnay – are. Given that ageing a wine in oak barrels adds significantly to the cost of a wine, it is impressive that at under a fiver there are so many wines in this category to choose from.

Chardonnay, being the international star it is, can be found thriving in vineyards all around the globe, not just in its native France. If you like the Chardonnay taste, you can experiment with Chardonnays from different countries and note how the flavours change, and yet the family resemblance remains.

In France, the really interesting Chardonnays come from the Languedoc region, down in the south.

Australian Chardonnay makes consistently good, fully blown wines. You can rarely go wrong with them if you are looking for a real mouthful of flavour. New Zealand Chardonnays tend to be slightly more austere, less up-front, and often more complex. South Africa is now producing some great Chardonnays, lighter in style than the former two countries' and full of tangy whitecurrant fruit.

But Chardonnay is not the only grape to produce full-bodied whites. The almost unknown Spanish Viura grape produces rich, unusually nutty whites in Rioja. If you fancy something totally different, you can even try a full-bodied Fumé Blanc (made from the Sauvignon Blanc grape) from Mexico!

Full-bodied whites are perfect with food. The added oakiness in many of them means they can cope with fairly strongly flavoured dishes, especially barbecued, char-grilled and smoked meats and fish. Creamy sauces can kill many a wine, but oak-aged, full-bodied whites – many of which have rich, creamy aromas and flavours – will cope admirably. Spicy food like Thai, Indian and Chinese cuisine calls for full-bodied whites, as does any dish spiked with lots of herbs, chillies or garlic.

Certain strong cheeses, like mature Cheddar, can taste surprisingly good with rich Chardonnay, perhaps not quite so surprising when you consider how well a white wine goes with a savoury dish topped with cheese.

Light Reds

It's easy to overlook light reds as people tend automatically to serve white when they are drinking an aperitif or eating a light dish. But light red can make a refreshing change, especially when chilled.

Light reds are wines with lots of juicy fruitiness and not too much bitter tannin. They include Beaujolais, made from the juicy Gamay grape, and several other wines made from similar varieties or by the same method (carbonic maceration). Sadly, many of the straight Beaujolais wines in the *Check it Out* tastings were disappointing. Pay just a few pence more for a Beaujolais-Villages and you'll be impressed by the difference.

Bulgaria offers some stunning value for money with its Merlot and Pinot Noir blends, wines which are light, fragrant and fruity, quite different in style to the well known, much more beefy Cabernet Sauvignons. If you like this style, look out also for light reds from Hungary.

Other countries worth trying include Germany, Italy (for Valpolicella and others), Argentina (for light, spicy Malbec) and Portugal, whose widely available bargain buy is a wine called Leziria.

While you can drink these wines on their own, they also go well with food. Serve them with salads, herby pizzas, pasta, light white fish, chicken, turkey, cheese and onion pie, mild cheese, sausages and mash, barbecues and picnics.

Medium-Bodied Reds

If you like claret or Rioja you'll enjoy any of the wines found in the Medium-Bodied Red sections. There are literally hundreds to choose from; this is by far the biggest category of red wines for sale in Britain. France produces both good and poor wines in this style. As well as a few Bordeaux Supérieur clarets that creep into this book by a whisker at £4.99, there are other neighbouring wines worth making a note of, in particular the aptly named Buzet, Côtes de Bourg and Côtes de Duras. Also look for Cabernet Sauvignon or Merlot-based wines produced further south in the Languedoc region. Fitou, Corbières, Minervois and Côtes du Roussillon are all good southern French bets too.

I found many of the Côtes du Rhônes, some of France's best selling reds, to be very mixed in quality in the *Check it Out* tastings, again proving that the mass sellers are rarely the best buys. Though there are some that are recommended, many were very disappointing. Crozes-Hermitage and Vin de Pays d'Hérault are better bets.

As with other best sellers, the Chiantis from Italy did not show well. Far better to chance your tastebuds with an Italian Merlot, Montepulciano or a Sicilian red which are much more consistent in quality.

Spain was impressive, not for its range of well known Riojas, but for the consistency of the stunning blackcurranty, plummy reds from Valdepeñas. They provide unbeatable value and flavour for money.

If you want to try something out of the ordinary, try Cabernet from Moldova or Romanian Merlot.

As regards food, the list is endless: roast beef, lamb, turkey, stews and casseroles, pasta and pizza, cheese and so on. But it is important not too serve too strongly flavoured dishes like game or anything too spicy with a medium-bodied red or it will swamp the flavour.

Full-Bodied Reds

Full-bodied reds have masses of fruit flavour and lots of tannin. They are a real mouthful and, if drunk without food, they can sometimes leave an unpleasantly bitter taste in the mouth. But with the right kind of fully flavoured dishes, they are delicious.

You'll enjoy full-bodied reds if you like rich, full clarets and big Australian and California wines. At this price level, Australia provides the most consistently high quality: like rich, rounded, spicy Shiraz and full, blackcurranty Cabernet Sauvignons.

Once you've met the Cabernet Sauvignon grape in Australia, you can follow it around the world. Start with Bulgaria, whose wines have an earthy, rustic sort of charm and which rarely disappoint, and then move on to Chile where the fruit flavours become more plummy and even richer.

California, who until recently had few wines costing under £5, came up with some respectable wines in this category.

When buying Italian, it is well worth trying out some wines with perhaps unfamiliar names such as Copertino, a rich red with vanilla, peppery overtones and masses of fruitiness, and the intriguingly named Anglianico del Vulture.

The most disappointing wines in this category under a fiver are the best known ones like Rioja. Look elsewhere in Spain and be adventurous – try one of those recommended in *Check it Out*, like Toro or Tempranillo, even if you have not heard of them.

France is a very mixed bag. Overall, the quality of full-bodied Côtes du Rhônes at this price level is poor. It's far better to look to lesser known areas in the south of France, especially *vin de pays* wines from the Oc.

If it is something completely different and completely unconventional you are after, try the rich, full-bodied sweet red from Greece, Mavrodaphne of Patras, from Morrisons. I've never tasted anything quite like it.

To show these wines at their best, match them with equally strongly flavoured food. Anything with lots of spices, herbs or garlic in it is ideal; so are chilli, Indian and southern French Provençal dishes. Rich, hearty stews and casseroles are good partners to full-bodied reds, as are any dishes which contain a lot of reduced wine, which is so concentrated it can knock many a medium-bodied red for six.

Well hung game, like pheasant, grouse and venison goes well with full-bodied red, especially wines made from the Syrah grape (or Shiraz as the Australians know it).

Strong Cheddar, soft, runny French cheese like Brie, goat's cheese and blue cheeses all have the right depth of flavour to complement rich, full reds.

Some of the slightly sweeter reds, like those from Australia and the south of France find a strange but successful partner in rich chocolate or coffee-based puddings which can smother many other wines, even the sweetest whites.

Sweet Whites

Ignore people who say they don't like sweet white! Perhaps they have never tasted a really good one. *Check it Out* will change all that. Chilled, a glass of any of the sweet whites included in this book, drunk either as an unusual aperitif or with food, is guaranteed to reach the parts other wines can't! The secret of really good sweet wines is that, while having luscious natural grape sugar, they also have enough balancing acidity to stop them tasting dull and cloying.

The main players in this section are French Sauternes taste-alikes, more elegant German wines, and blockbusting, alcoholic, Spanish Muscats.

All sweet wines need to be served really chilled. Some, especially the Muscats (or Moscatels), are so rich that a bottle is enough to serve 12 people. Many also have handy screw-tops and can be kept in the fridge for a few weeks without serious deterioration.

You can liven up a dinner party by serving a glass of sweet wine with the starter – as is often done in

France. It is an unusual complement to rich pâté, game soup and strong fish, like mackerel. It also goes well with strong blue cheese (Roquefort and Sauternes is a classic combination) or any dish cooked with strong cheese. And of course, it tastes wonderful with any type of pudding or cake.

Sparkling Wines

There is nothing like a bottle of bubbly to create an instant party atmosphere. And today that does not have to mean expensive champagne. The sparkling wines included in *Check it Out* are of a remarkably high quality, especially when one considers the costly, time consuming production methods involved. Champagne-makers will have to look to their laurels if this is the kind of quality one can get for under a fiver.

The Spanish cavas, produced in the Penedès district of Spain, are of an exceptional standard. Made using the same method as for champagne, these wines have lots of complexity and moreish dry fruit. They make ideal aperitifs and, because of their depth of flavour, will go well with food too. Cava and roast chicken are a great combination.

Australia makes consistently good quality dry fizz, without the same complexity as cava, but nonetheless eminently drinkable and suitable for every celebration. Both the Spanish and these Australian sparklers far out-classed French wines in the *Check it Out* tastings.

The quality of Asti, Italy's popular fizz, has improved dramatically over the last few years. Its aromatic, medium-dry grapiness is what makes is so versatile and appealing. While it makes for an ideal aperitif, particularly during the summer, it has enough floral fruit flavour to complement cakes and puddings too.

Lambrusco is cheap and cheerful and today better made than ever. It has the added advantage of being low in alcohol (normally around 5%), so is a good thirst quencher and an ideal summer garden quaffing wine, or great for a party or picnic. As it is medium-sweet, it will please all those who find dry sparklers too tart.

To show at their best, all these bubblies should be served well chilled.

Rosé

A few years ago, the rosé section of any tasting was enough to drive you to drink. Well, anything other than rosé! Today, winemaking has improved wildly and there are many decent ones from which to choose.

There are many more too, than the old favourite, sickly sweet Anjou Rosé – although there are two excellent Anjou Rosés listed here. There are now quality dry rosés from Bordeaux as well as southern France and Provence, and delicious wines from places as far flung as Hungary and California.

Because there are now so many different styles, from light- to full-bodied, rosé has become much more versatile, and is no longer a wine to be confined to sunny, hot summer days. Instead, be adventurous, serve it as an all-year-round aperitif, and try it with dishes like salad, cheese, cold meats, roasted white meats like chicken and turkey, pasta, pizza and lamb.

Fuller-bodied rosés, those that tend to be darker in colour, like Bordeaux Clairet – which has all the fruit character of claret without the tannin – can be treated like medium-bodied reds and therefore go with many more dishes.

Go for pink when you can't decide between white and red – it makes for a refreshing change both to the eye and the palate. And always serve it chilled.

ASDA

★★★ STAR BUYS ★★★

Chardonnay, Private Reserve, Mecsekalji, 1992

■ £2.99 ■ Hungary ■ Star White

Crisp, clean, almost gooseberry-like dry white with a flowery aroma and tangy, rounded fruit flavours. A stylish, easy-drinking white, guaranteed to please all. Great with vegetarian dishes or as an aperitif.

Anglianico del Vulture, Carbone, 1987

■ £4.99 ■ Italy ■ Star Red

Elegant aromas of vanilla and cherry coupled with lots of violet flavour and good tannin make this an extraordinarily complex wine for the money. Try serving it with spicy sausages, beef stew or peppered steak.

Wines by Style

LIGHT DRY WHITE

Chardonnay, Private Reserve, Mecsekalji, 1992

■ £2.99 ■ Hungary

Crisp, clean, almost gooseberry-like dry white with a flowery aroma and tangy, rounded fruit flavours. A stylish, easy-drinking wine, guaranteed to please all. Great with vegetarian dishes or as an aperitif.

Douro White, Asda

■ £2.99 ■ Portugal

An unusual, rustic, earthy white with herbal overtones and an attractive lemony zip on the finish. Goes well with creamy fish dishes or herby omelettes.

Entre-Deux-Mers, Château Fondarzac, 1992

■ £3.95 ■ France

Crisp and dry with gooseberry overtones. Quite luscious fruit flavours too. Drink as an aperitif.

Muscadet de Sèvre-et-Maine Sur Lie, Bossard, (Organic), 1992

■ £4.99 ■ France

This stylish white, with an attractive label, is worth paying extra for. Lots of appealingly crisp, yet floral fruit flavour combines with a yeasty, dry, slight creaminess. If someone says they don't like Muscadet, try them on this one.

Verdicchio, Asda

■ £3.29 ■ Italy

Good value for money with a slightly peppery aroma and tangy, honeysuckle fruit flavour. Good as an aperitif or serve it with light salads or soufflés.

Vin de Pays des Côtes de Gascogne, Domaines Grassa, Asda

■ £2.99 ■ France

This wine is consistently good, year in, year out. Crisp, sherbet-like fruit flavours are backed up by a tangy, fruity aftertaste. Goes surprisingly well with pork dishes.

MEDIUM-DRY WHITE

Niersteiner Rosenberg Riesling Kabinett, Graf Wolff Metternich, Rheinhessen, 1991

■ £4.79 ■ Germany

Sherbet fruit flavour with a refreshingly lemony tang. Try it with pancakes.

Niersteiner Spiegelberg Kabinett, Rudolf Muller, Asda, 1992

■ £2.99 ■ Germany

Floral flavoured party wine with a zippy, tangy finish.

Wiltinger Scharzberg Riesling Kabinett, Mosel, Asda, 1991

■ £2.99 ■ Germany

A crisp, appley wine with a honeyed sherbet aftertaste. Serve with fruit or apple crumble.

FULL-BODIED DRY WHITE

Chardonnay, Goundrey Langton, Mount Barker, Western Australia, 1992

■ £4.99 ■ Australia

This wine shows the complexity Western Australia is capable of: ripe, steely fruit aroma and stylish peachy, grapefruit flavours with a touch of oak. Very moreish. Ideal to serve with fish pâté, smoked salmon or Chinese food.

Chardonnay, Southeast Australia, Asda, 1992

■ £3.99 ■ Australia

Rich, buttery flavours with a lemony tang. Extremely drinkable. Serve with cheese-on-toast or anything with a cheese topping. Tastes good with mature cheddar.

Semillon-Chardonnay, Southeast Australia, Asda, 1992

■ £3.29 ■ Australia

A lightly spiced aperitif wine with a refreshing, zippy, moreish fruitiness. Drink ultra-chilled.

LIGHT RED

Cape Red, Clearsprings, Simonsvlei

■ £2.85 ■ South Africa

A fruity, easy-drinking red with soft, lightly spicy, rounded fruit flavour. Drink on its own or with soup, sandwiches or salad. Excellent value for money.

Kékfrankos, Hungary, 1992

■ £2.69 ■ Hungary

At this price don't worry if you've never heard of the Kékfrankos grape, try it anyway. Light, spicy and moreish, with earthy overtones. Drink on its own, or with salads, bacon sandwiches or honey-roast ham.

Merlot, Villány, Hungary, 1991

■ £2.69 ■ Hungary

Ripe cherry aroma, followed by light, delicate violet flavours and a tang of acidity. Easy-drinking party wine.

Vintages and Prices
Whilst every care has been taken to ensure that vintages and prices of wines detailed in *Check it Out* are the same as those on sale, it is possible that some will have changed. If a more recent vintage is in stock, the quality should be comparable, and therefore a similar buy. (With the majority of whites, especially light and medium-dry whites, a rule of thumb is 'the younger the vintage, the fresher the wine'.)

St-Chinian, Asda

■ £2.85 ■ France

Earthy, plummy red from the village of the same name in Languedoc-Roussillon. An easy-drinking, good value, party wine. Serve with pasta or pizza.

Valencia Red, Asda

■ £2.39 ■ Spain

Look for the stylish black label with a chilli on it. Fruity, earthy, moreish – a party red.

MEDIUM-BODIED RED

Sangiovese della Marche, Asda

■ £3.49 ■ Italy

Masses of ripe, peppery fruitiness. Easy-drinking, a good all-rounder. Ideal with any light supper.

FULL-BODIED RED

Anglianico del Vulture, Carbone, 1987

■ £4.99 ■ Italy

Elegant aromas of vanilla and cherry coupled with

lots of violet flavour and good tannin make this an extraordinarily complex wine for the money. Good with spicy sausages, beef stew or peppered steak.

Barbera d'Asti, Cantine Gemma, 1990

■ £4.49 ■ Italy

Lots of strawberry fruit with attractive underlying bitter tannin flavours make this wine alarmingly easy to drink. Towards the lighter side of full-bodied – ideal with bolognese-type pasta dishes.

Cirò Rosso Classico, Librandi, 1991

■ £3.99 ■ Italy

Honest, straightforward Italian red with rustic, cherry-like flavours. Great served with a pepperoni pizza.

Corbières, Château de Cabriac, 1991

■ £3.29 ■ France

Attractively fresh and fruity and full of flavour, conjuring up visions of hot southern French sun. Excellent with spicy cold meats like salami.

SWEET WHITE

Moscatel de Valencia, Asda

■ £2.95 ■ Spain

Enticing barley sugar aromas and rich, marmalade-like flavour make this a very moreish (and strong at 15% alcohol) sweet white. Produced in southeast Spain. The screw-top bottle makes it easy to keep in the fridge where, once opened, it will last for at least two weeks (if you can resist it) without deteriorating.

Delicious with creamy, fruity puddings. The stylish grey label means it will look smart in the very best company.

Muscat, Vin de Table, Henry Peyrottes

■ £3.49 ■ France

Sold in handy clear screw-top bottles, this southern French Muscat produced near Sète has a strong, perfumed, grapey aroma and sweet, violet-like fruit. So moreish it's easy to forget its strength of 15% alcohol. Drink with puddings, or ultra-cold as an aperitif.

DRY SPARKLING WHITE

Cava, Asda

■ £4.99 ■ Spain

This is a really attractive bubbly, both to the eye and palate. Bottled in a stylish bulbous bottle with a classy green label, it has lots of yeasty, rounded fruit flavour with a crisp, dry finish. Good enough for any occasion.

BUDGENS

★★★ STAR BUYS ★★★

Flonheimer Adelberg Auslese, 1992

■ £3.99 ■ Germany ■ Star White

This Rheinhessen wine has an attractive floral aroma and sweet, but not cloying, fruit flavour. A citrus bite on the finish masks some of the sweetness, making it extremely easy to drink. A very stylish wine which tastes as if it should cost twice its price. Drink chilled as an aperitif or with not too sweet, fruit-based puddings.

Valencia Reserva, Marqués de Caro, 1988

■ £3.45 ■ Spain ■ Star Red

A rich, luscious wine with hints of soft, fresh tobacco and lots of delicious, mouthwatering, cherry-like flavour. If you're into figures, each one of the 92,500 bottles produced is individually numbered.

Wines by Style

LIGHT DRY WHITE

Chardonnay, Varna Region

■ £3.05 ■ Bulgaria

A very floral wine with elderflower-like aromas. Unusually perfumed for Chardonnay. Produced in the Varna region, where it is drunk in the Black Sea ports with local fish.

Soave, Budgens

■ £3.15 ■ Italy

Light, floral, honeyed aromas are followed by zippy, sherbet-like dry fruit flavour with a hint of almonds. A wine to try with trout and almonds or a nutty risotto dish.

Surrey Gold, Denbies, 1990

■ £4.99 ■ England

Produced from England's largest vineyard with over 250 acres on the North Downs in Surrey. An attractive, fruity wine with a slightly honeyed aftertaste. Serve with baked ham and mushy peas.

MEDIUM-DRY WHITE

Bereich Bernkastel, Peter Mertes, 1992

■ £2.99 ■ Germany

An appealingly flowery white with off-dry flavours of elderflowers and a good tang of acidity on the finish. A refreshing aperitif.

Erben Kabinett, Franz Wihl. Langguth, 1992

■ £3.99 ■ Germany

Smells and tastes like pineapple chunks! Drink as an aperitif or with sweet-and-sour dishes.

Liebfraumilch, Rheinhessen, Budgens

■ £2.59 ■ Germany

A floral, zippy wine with a delicious, crisp, lemony aftertaste. Good for drinking anytime.

FULL-BODIED DRY WHITE

Chardonnay, Proprietor's Reserve, Glen Ellen, 1992

■ £4.55 ■ USA

An attractive spicy aroma with rich, slightly smoky fruit flavour on the palate. Excellent value for money. Good party wine.

Côtes de Saint Mont, Tuilerie du Bosc

■ £3.99 ■ France

Produced 100 miles south of Bordeaux, this wine comes from a vineyard site first planted by Benedictine monks in the 11th Century. Of course, the present vines are not quite that old, but the wine none the less has an impressively rich aroma: slightly gingery, with a touch of citrus. On the palate the fruit is soft and lightly caramely. Try drinking this one with spiced potted shrimps.

Semillon, Rainbow Fields, Riverina Wines, Southeast Australia

■ £3.45 ■ Australia

Attractive aperitif wine with lime overtones and a slightly smoky fruit flavour. It tastes good with stir-fried prawns.

LIGHT RED

Leziria Tinto

■ £2.59 ■ Portugal

Excellent value for money. Produced northeast of

Lisbon, this wine has an earthy, raspberry aroma and soft, creamy, raspberry fruitiness to the taste with a good tang of acidity. An anytime-drinking party red; can be drunk chilled too.

MEDIUM-BODIED RED

Cabernet Sauvignon, Vin de Pays des Sables du Golfe du Lion, Domaine de Bosquet Canet, 1990

■ £4.19 ■ France

Organically produced, stylish southern red with lots of structure. Ripe blackcurrants and creamy flavours that linger for ages. Ideal with game or strong cheese, especially Stilton.

Coteaux Varois, Abbaye St-Hilaire, 1991

■ £3.35 ■ France

Delicious peppery aromas and tasty, spicy, plummy fruitiness. This wine goes well with spicy dishes like chicken with black bean sauce, beef curry or with lamb Madras.

Crozes-Hermitage, Les Ramières, 1991

■ £4.69 ■ France

Easy-drinking and rounded, with spicy, jammy, tangy fruit flavours. Try serving it with roast beef or steak sandwiches.

Pinot Noir, Underraga, Maipo Valley, 1991

■ £4.99 ■ Chile

Rich, smoky aroma and ripe strawberry flavour with

a hint of black pepper. Soft and rounded, serve with roast lamb.

FULL-BODIED RED

Charbono, Inglenook, Napa, 1985

■ £4.99 ■ USA

Intense purple colour with a rich smell of plums and black cherries. This is an earthy, tannic red with a touch of vanilla on the finish. Would go well with any dish using rosemary, thyme and/or garlic.

Rioja, Gran Reserva, Gran Condal, 1981

■ £4.99 ■ Spain

A ripe, mature, soft, vanilla-flavoured wine with concentrated plummy character. Full-bodied, yet soft and velvety. Delicious with roast pork or lamb. Stunning for its price.

Valencia Reserva, Marqués de Caro, 1988

■ £3.45 ■ Spain

A rich, luscious wine with hints of soft, fresh tobacco and lots of delicious, mouthwatering, cherry-like flavour. If you're into figures, each one of the 92,500 bottles of Valencia Reserva produced annually is individually numbered.

SWEET WHITE

Flonheimer Adelberg Auslese, 1992

■ £3.99 ■ Germany

This Rheinhessen wine has an attractive floral

aroma and sweet, but not cloying, fruit flavour. A citrus bite on the finish masks some sweetness, making it extremely easy to drink. A very stylish wine which tastes as if it should cost twice its price. Drink chilled as an aperitif or with not too sweet, fruit-based puddings.

DRY ROSE

Vin de Pays des Sables du Golfe du Lion, Gris de Gris, Listel, 1992

■ £3.85 ■ France

Barely pink, this wine is organically produced in the sand-dunes of the Camargue. It is light and elegant with an attractive earthy fruit flavour. Ideal with seafood, especially prawns and shrimps.

DRY SPARKLING WHITE

Flinders Creek, Brut

■ £4.99 ■ Australia

Crisp, clean and fruity, this is a fizz for those who like theirs really dry. An ideal aperitif.

DRY SPARKLING ROSE

Rosé, Flinders Creek

■ £4.99 ■ Australia

Day-glo pink in colour, with an appealing aroma of rose petals. Rounded fruit (just like raspberry ripple ice-cream) on the palate makes this very moreish. Excellent quality for the price.

SWEET SPARKLING ROSE

Lambrusco Blush

■ £2.59 ■ Italy

It's easy to recognize this wine because of its distinctive, flowery, slanting strip label. Masses of strawberry-like, sweet fizz makes it the ideal accompaniment to plain red fruit or fruit tart.

Vintages and Prices

Whilst every care has been taken to ensure that vintages and prices of wines detailed in *Check it Out* are the same as those on sale, it is possible that some will have changed. If a more recent vintage is in stock, the quality should be comparable, and therefore a similar buy. (With the majority of whites, especially light and medium-dry whites, a rule of thumb is 'the younger the vintage, the fresher the wine'.)

CO-OP

★★★ STAR BUYS ★★★

Chardonnay, Preslav, Bulgarian, Co-op

■ £2.99 ■ Bulgaria ■ Star White

This is a crisp, zippy white with a flavour of Granny Smith apples. An excellent value, easy-drinking wine. Serve with veal, chicken or turkey.

Valpolicella, Co-op

■ £2.99 ■ Italy ■ Star Red

A light, creamy red with cherry overtones. Easy-drinking anytime, and especially good for picnics. A good all-rounder. Tastes good chilled.

Wines by Style

LIGHT DRY WHITE

Chardonnay, Preslav, Bulgarian, Co-op

■ £2.99 ■ Bulgaria

This is a crisp, zippy white with a flavour of Granny Smith apples. An excellent value, easy-drinking wine. Serve with veal, chicken or turkey.

Frascati, Co-op, 1993

■ £3.39 ■ Italy

A gluggable dry white with a lightly yeasty taste. Serve as aperitif or with salads or pasta.

Pinot Blanc, Alsace, Co-op

■ £4.55 ■ France

Lightly honeyed aroma, with a rounded, tangy flavour and a hint of spice on the finish. Very quaffable. Serve with meat in a fruit sauce or as an aperitif.

Vin de Pays des Côtes de Gascogne, Co-op

■ £2.99 ■ France

Produced in the Armagnac area of France, this wine has a curious minty quality and perfumed vanilla fruitiness. Serve with herby fish dishes or mushroom risotto.

MEDIUM-DRY WHITE

Vinho Verde, Co-op

■ £3.09 ■ Portugal

An easy-drinking white in a distinctive dumpy bottle. Its light spritz makes it very refreshing, as does its attractive appley aftertaste. Best drunk as an aperitif.

LIGHT RED

Valencia Red, Co-op

■ £2.49 ■ Spain

An earthy, lightly spicy red with rough-and-ready flavour. Drink chilled with pasta, pizzas and paella.

Valpolicella, Co-op

■ £2.99 ■ Italy

A light, creamy red with cherry overtones. Easily drinkable and especially good for picnics. Good chilled.

MEDIUM-BODIED RED

Bergerac Rouge, Co-op

■ £3.25 ■ France

You've heard of the detective, so get to know the wine of the same name, produced to the east of the Bordeaux region. Made from the same grapes as claret – Cabernet Sauvignon and Merlot – this has good liquorice flavour and lots of rich, full-bodied, quite austere fruitiness. Great with strong cheese.

Cabernet Sauvignon, Vin de Pays d'Oc, Co-op

■ £3.29 ■ France

A very perfumed wine with masses of violet and blackcurrant-like, soft Mediterranean fruit character. Ideal with herby, garlic-laced, Provence-style food.

Claret, Co-op

■ £2.99 ■ France

Good, straightforward, well-priced Bordeaux red with a liquoricy aroma and easy-drinking, softish blackcurrant flavour. Ideal with roast lamb, pork or beef.

Corbières, Co-op

■ £2.79 ■ France

A pleasant, jammy, easy-drinking wine with ripe, softly plummy fruit character. Serve with steak and chips.

Fitou, Co-op

■ £3.45 ■ France

Lots of jamminess and earthy, rounded, autumn fruit

flavour on the finish make this a good all-rounder. Drink with roast chicken, turkey, beef or lamb.

Minervois, Co-op

■ £2.99 ■ France

A full-flavoured, blackberry-like wine. Good with garlic mushrooms or cheese on toast. A party wine.

Navarra Tinto, Co-op

■ £2.99 ■ Spain

Rough-and-ready spicy red from Rioja's less known neighbour. Good with garlicky dishes or roast pork.

Rioja Tinto, Bodegas Almenar, Co-op

■ £3.79 ■ Spain

Soft, rounded, cherry-flavoured red wine with hints of sweet tobacco and vanilla. Try serving it with roast lamb or pork.

Sicilian Red, Co-op

■ £2.89 ■ Italy

A perfumed, soft, party red full of tangy, plummy flavours. A great all-rounder.

FULL-BODIED RED

Dão, Co-op, 1990

■ £2.99 ■ Portugal

A fairly rustic wine with cherry overtones and masses of earthy flavour. Great value. Would make any everyday supper like bangers and mash taste good.

Ruby Cabernet, California, Co-op

■ £3.49 ■ USA

While the back label says 'soft, easy-drinking' this is in fact a rich, full-bodied red. It has a distinct smell of eucalyptus and lots of tarry, punch-packing black cherry flavour. Serve with spicy food or strong cheese.

SWEET SPARKLING WHITE

Light White, Co-op

■ £1.99 ■ Germany

With less than 2% alcohol, you can serve this lightly fizzy, honeyed white to those who don't want to drink much, or have to drive. Ideal for mixing half and half with orange juice for Buck's Fizz.

Moscato Spumante, Co-op

■ £3.69 ■ Italy

Spicy, grapey fruit flavour and a refreshing gentle fizz make this eminently gluggable – and not too potent, at just 4.5% alcohol. Its handy screw-top means you can keep the bottle in the fridge for up to two weeks before the wine deteriorates. Serve with fruit salad.

SWEET ROSE

Rosé d'Anjou, Co-op

■ £2.99 ■ France

There's lots of ripe, cherry-like sweet fruit flavour in this well-known Loire Valley rosé, with a tangy, long-lingering finish. Much tastier than most of its type.

GATEWAY

★★★ STAR BUYS ★★★

Cava, Blanc de Blancs, Conde de Caralt, Somerfield

■ £4.99 ■ Spain ■ Star White

Produced in northeastern Spain not far from Barcelona, this stylish, floral bubbly has creamy, appley overtones on the finish. Much greater complexity than many more expensive champagnes. A great party wine, serve chilled.

Corbières, Château de Caraguilhes, 1990

■ £4.25 ■ France ■ Star Red

Deliciously full-bodied (but without too much tannin) and with masses of soft, yet mouth-filling, liquorice-like, peppery fruit flavour. This organically produced, affordable red looks good too in its stylish painted bottle. Serve with strongly flavoured pâté or steak and kidney pie.

Wines by Style

LIGHT DRY WHITE

Australian Dry White, Somerfield

■ £3.19 ■ Australia

Unusual spicy, citrusy white; dry, yet lightly luscious. Drink with roast chicken.

Baden Dry, Badischer Winzerkeller, Somerfield

■ £3.29 ■ Germany

Flowery dry white with clean, fresh fruit flavour, from the sunny south of Germany. Its soft, yet dry style means few could dislike it. Drink anytime.

Bourgogne, White Burgundy, T Jouvet, Somerfield

■ £4.89 ■ France

Attractive, rich, lightly buttery white with stylish dry fruitiness and a slightly toasted aftertaste. Serve with smoked salmon, smoked chicken or roast chicken.

Chardonnay, Mór Region, Hungarian, Somerfield, 1992

■ £2.99 ■ Hungary

This wine's stylish label and flavour belie its very reasonable price. It has a floral aroma and dry, easy-drinking fruit flavours. Will appeal to all: a great party wine, great value.

Frascati, Somerfield, 1992

■ £3.75 ■ Italy

The attractive perfumed aroma is followed by crisp fruitiness and a lively tang of acidity in this wine. Could cope with quite oily fish, like sardines.

Mâcon Blanc-Villages, 1992

■ £4.49 ■ France

Zippy, flinty white with rich flavours and a lingering aftertaste. Serve with chicken, turkey or guinea-fowl.

Muscadet de Sèvre-et-Maine, J Beauquin, Somerfield, 1992

■ £2.99 ■ France

Lightly floral, with an attractive dry, fruity taste and a slightly appley prickle on the finish. What you save on the wine, spend on the oysters!

Pinot Blanc Trocken, St-Ursula, 1992

■ £3.45 ■ Germany

A soft, rounded, lightly spicy German white finishing with a lemony tang. Serve with savoury pancakes.

Riesling Trocken, Rheinpfalz, Somerfield, 1989

■ £3.95 ■ Germany

Definitely an acquired taste. The rich, oily, marzipan-like aroma is followed by tangy, perfumed flavour and a citrus finish. An ideal foil for sweet-and-sour sauces.

Sauvignon, Haut-Poitou, 1991

■ £4.25 ■ France

Slightly tropical fruit aromas and delicious violet fruit on the palate. An unusual white, ideal with cod, lightly smoked fish and surprisingly good with goat's cheese.

Sauvignon Blanc, Peteroa, Chile, Somerfield, 1992

■ £3.55 ■ Chile

Produced in the Maipo Valley between the snow-capped Andes and the Pacific Ocean, this wine is fresh and zippy with a distinctive flavour of gooseberries. Drink with chicken or turkey.

Semillon-Chardonnay, Jacob's Creek, 1993

■ £4.29 ■ Australia

Widely available from many other stores, this is, deservedly, one of Britain's best selling whites. Lots of melon-like, dry fruit flavours, with slightly cordial-like notes. Good with barbecued and smoked food.

Soave, Somerfield, 1992

■ £2.99 ■ Italy

Soft, yet fresh fruit flavours. An easy-drinking party white which will not offend.

Trocken Rheinhessen, Somerfield

■ £3.15 ■ Germany

'Trocken' means dry and this wine combines dryness with an apple-and-pear flavour and a crisp, zippy, lemony aftertaste. Try serving it with chicken and mushroom pie.

Vin de Pays des Côtes de Gascogne, Domaines Grassa, Somerfield, 1992

■ £3.49 ■ France

Clean, crisp and refreshing with slightly peppery overtones and mouthwatering fruitiness. Drink on its own or with grilled fish or roast chicken.

Vino da Tavola di Sicilia, Montereale Bianco, Somerfield

■ £2.95 ■ Italy

Quite aromatic, gooseberry-like white with tangy, rounded fruit flavours. Ideal with fish and chips.

MEDIUM-DRY WHITE

Bereich Bernkasteler, R Müller, Somerfield

■ £2.79 ■ Germany

This Mosel wine is like flowery sherbet. Good with light fish dishes, try it with grilled plaice or Dover sole.

Chenin Blanc, Simonsvlei, 1993

■ £3.25 ■ South Africa

An attractive, lightly honeyed aroma with lots of deliciously refreshing peach flavour and a lemony, tangy finish. Good with prawns, scallops or potted shrimps.

Hock, R Müller, Somerfield

■ £2.39 ■ Germany

A flowery, easy-drinking wine, with an earthy, yeasty flavour. A good aperitif.

Liebfraumilch, Somerfield

■ £2.39 ■ Germany

Zippy, earthy white: pleasantly fruity, gluggable and moreish. Serve it with chicken salad or with corn on the cob.

Mainzer Domherr Kabinett, Rheinhessen, Somerfield, 1991

■ £3.19 ■ Germany

Produced near Mainz, this has zippy, earthy flavour with a hint of honeyed nuts on the finish. An excellent match for honey-roast ham, nut cutlets, or trout and almonds.

Morio Muskat, St-Ursula, Pfalz, 1992

■ £2.99 ■ Germany

Grapey aromas with soft, easy-drinking flavour and a herbal tang. Try with pasta and pesto or herby omelettes.

Riesling, Rheingau, 1992

■ £3.49 ■ Germany

Rich wine with flowery flavours and a lemony zing. Good with sardines or dishes laced with olive oil.

Riesling Kabinett, Mosel, Somerfield, 1990

■ £3.49 ■ Germany

Complex aromas and stylish, oily, appley flavours. Unusual. Serve with spicy prawns or potted shrimps.

Valencia Medium Dry White

■ £2.49 ■ Spain

Smells like mince-pies flavoured with caramelized pears. Great with sweet-and-sour dishes or fruit salad.

Vouvray, Somerfield, 1992

■ £3.49 ■ France

Look for the church on the label. A great all-rounder and a refreshingly different aperitif: zippy, tangy, floral.

FULL-BODIED DRY WHITE

Bordeaux Blanc, (Oak Aged), Eschenauer, 1991

■ £4.25 ■ France

If the only Bordeaux you normally drink is red, this is

the white to change all that. Rich vanilla aromas are followed by smoky, creamy, vanilla fruit flavours. Ideal with creamy pasta dishes and veal.

Chardonnay, Australian, Southeast Australia, Somerfield

■ £4.25 ■ Australia

Produced in the southeast of Australia, this has an attractive, lightly honeyed aroma and lots of dry, zippy fruit flavour. Drink it with smoked salmon or chicken.

Chardonnay, Jacob's Creek, Orlando, Southeast Australia, 1993

■ £4.29 ■ Australia

Much more impressive than the 1992 vintage, this best selling white smells like bananas and cream and has a tangy floral flavour on the finish. An anytime drinking wine.

Chardonnay, Koonunga Hill, Penfolds, Southeast Australia, 1992

■ £4.99 ■ Australia

A strong vanilla aroma is backed up by rich, buttery fruit flavour with a zippy, lemony tang. Serve this wine with cassoulet, roast or stir-fried chicken, or chicken soup.

Chardonnay, Sebastiani

■ £3.99 ■ USA

A gutsy, quite austere wine with spicy overtones; reminiscent of a good Chablis. Serve with spicy food.

LIGHT RED

Bardolino, Somerfield

■ £2.99 ■ Italy

A light, easy-drinking red wine from the southern shores of Lake Garda. Smells of bubblegum, with lots of spicy, tangy fruit flavour. Ideal with spicy pizzas and tastes good chilled too.

Beaujolais, Somerfield, 1992

■ £3.69 ■ France

Lots of rounded juicy flavours. Very drinkable, just as good Beaujolais should be. Serve chilled as an aperitif or with light omelettes, salads or bacon sandwiches.

Beaujolais-Villages, Jean Gamet, 1992

■ £4.45 ■ France

A cut above the average Beaujolais with a ripe, fruity bouquet and lots of moreish red fruit flavour. A delicious complement to *coq au vin* or *boeuf bourguignon.*

Dornfelder, St-Ursula, 1992

■ £3.99 ■ Germany

An unusual light, easy-drinking red, with ripe, plummy aromas and refreshing tangy plum flavour. Serve chilled. Good with casseroles and cold meats.

Leziria Tinto

■ £2.49 ■ Portugal

This is brilliant value for money. Produced northeast of Lisbon, it has an earthy, raspberry aroma and soft, creamy, raspberry flavours with a good tang of acidity. An anytime-drinking party red; can be drunk chilled.

Merlot-Pinot Noir, Bulgarian Country Wine, Sliven

■ £2.65 ■ Bulgaria

Attractive chocolate and plum aromas with a taste of lightly spiced, plummy fruit. An easy-drinking, great value wine. Makes cheese on toast far more exciting.

Planicie Tinto

■ £2.99 ■ Portugal

Don't worry if you've never tasted a Portuguese red, this is a good one to start with: it has ripe, roasted, raspberry aromas and a rounded, creamy flavour, with oaky sweetness on the finish. Great with roast lamb.

Vino da Tavola del Veneto, Caldeo Rosso, Somerfield, 1991

■ £2.85 ■ Italy

An unusual aroma of earthy, very perfumed violets, with lots of soft, easy-drinking fruit flavour. Very more-ish. Serve as an aperitif or with light pasta dishes.

MEDIUM-BODIED RED

Buzet, Renaissance, Somerfield, 1991

■ £3.75 ■ France

Soft, gluggable wine which lives up to its name (sounds like 'boozy'!). Even people who don't normally like red might enjoy a glass of this one. Excellent with cassoulet or Chinese-style stir-fry beef dishes.

Cabernet Sauvignon, Chile, Somerfield, 1992

■ £3.35 ■ Chile

A ripe, plummy wine with rich, blackcurrant fruit flavour. Try it with duck or goose.

Cabernet Sauvignon, Vin de Pays d'Oc, Somerfield

■ £2.99 ■ France

Peppery aromas and rounded, earthy, curranty flavours make this red the ideal foil for char-grilled or barbecued food. Buy in a few bottles, it's a real bargain.

California Dry Red, Somerfield

■ £3.45 ■ USA

Irresistible, perfumed red with spicy blackcurrant flavour. Serve with creamy chicken dishes or spicy beef.

Chianti, Conti Serristori, Somerfield, 1992

■ £3.29 ■ Italy

Amazing aromas of plums and cherries make this impossible to resist. The flavour is no disappointment either: rich, ripe, pepperiness and luscious chocolate on the finish. Serve with bangers and mash or game.

Vintages and Prices

Whilst every care has been taken to ensure that vintages and prices of wines detailed in *Check it Out* are the same as those on sale, it is possible that some will have changed. If a more recent vintage is in stock, the quality should be comparable, and therefore a similar buy. (With the majority of whites, especially light and medium-dry whites, a rule of thumb is 'the younger the vintage, the fresher the wine'.)

Claret, Eschenauer, Somerfield

■ £2.99 ■ France

Good value Bordeaux with soft, rounded, easy-drinking fruit flavour. Ideal to serve with roast chicken, turkey or lamb.

Côtes de Duras, 1992

■ £3.19 ■ France

This region lies to the east of the city of Bordeaux and produces excellent red wines. Attractive red fruit aromas with easy-to-drink, soft (not tannic) fruit on the palate. Try serving it with creamy soups, stews or casseroles.

Merlot, Stambolovo Reserve, Haskovo, 1987

■ £3.49 ■ Bulgaria

Seductive aroma, like an old mature claret; soft, rounded fruit flavour and a balancing tang of acidity on the finish. Try it with duck or goose.

Merlot, Vin de Pays des Collines de la Moure, Domaine de la Magdelaine, 1991

■ £3.25 ■ France

A soft, ripe wine with attractive chocolate aromas and light, roasted flavour. Good with guinea-fowl, chicken roasted with garlic, or spicy pizza.

Montereale, Sicilian Red, Somerfield

■ £2.99 ■ Italy

Spicy, easy-drinking red with earthy, plummy flavour. Drink with barbecued or char-grilled meat.

Shiraz-Cabernet Sauvignon, Australian Dry Red, Southeast Australia, Somerfield

■ £3.19 ■ Australia

Smooth, gulpable red with ripe blackcurrant flavour. Ideal with barbecues or char-grilled meat.

South African Pinotage, 1993

■ £3.25 ■ South Africa

Ripe and spicy with lots of mouthwatering fruitiness, a good all-rounder red to brighten up any dull supper.

Valdepeñas, Señorio de Val, Cencibel, Casa de la Viña, 1988

■ £2.99 ■ Spain

This area of Spain produces excellent value-for-money reds, bursting with blackcurrant flavour. This one tastes as if it should cost more than a fiver.

Valpolicella, Somerfield

■ £2.99 ■ Italy

An irresistible perfumed red with floral, violet flavours. A great party wine; could be served chilled.

Vin de Pays des Côtes de Gascogne, 1992

■ £2.89 ■ France

From an area better known for white wine. Lots of ripe, earthy flavour makes it easy-drinking anytime.

Vin de Pays de l'Hérault, Domaine de St-Julien

■ £2.79 ■ France

A simple, fruity wine with spicy, blackcurrant flavour. Serve with cold meats like salami or spicy pizza.

FULL-BODIED RED

Cabernet Sauvignon Reserva, Santa Rita, 1989

■ £4.99 ■ Chile

Spicy and rich with concentrated blackcurrant fruit character that lingers on and on. Could even cope with beef and horseradish.

Corbières, Château de Caraguilhes, 1990

■ £4.25 ■ France

Deliciously full-bodied, not too tannic, and with masses of soft, yet mouth-filling, liquorice-like, peppery flavour. Organically produced affordable red that looks good too in its stylish painted bottle. Serve with strongly flavoured pâté or steak and kidney pie.

Corbières, Val d'Orbieu, Somerfield, 1992

■ £2.99 ■ France

A soft, irresistible red, with the ripeness of flavour one expects from southern France. Alarmingly easy to drink and not too heavy to drink on its own.

Côtes du Rhône, Domaine de la Solitude, 1991

■ £4.25 ■ France

One of the stars of the *Check it Out* tastings, this has an intensely perfumed aroma, and masses of rich, plummy, spicy chocolate on the palate. It tastes delicious with game or any meat with a rich wine sauce.

Fitou, Les Producteurs de Mont Tauch, Somerfield

■ £3.35 ■ France

This popular southern French wine is still great value. It smells of vanilla and has intense blackcurrant-like flavour. Ideal with any dish laced with herbs and garlic.

Shiraz, Australia, Somerfield

■ £3.99 ■ Australia

Rich, roasted, meaty aromas and masses of plummy, full-bodied, spicy flavour. Serve with barbecued food.

DRY SPARKLING WHITE

Cava, Blanc de Blancs, Conde de Caralt, Somerfield

■ £4.99 ■ Spain

From near Barcelona, this stylish, floral bubbly has a creamy, appley finish. Much greater complexity than many champagnes. A great party wine, serve chilled.

Great Western Brut Reserve, Seppelt

■ £4.99 ■ Australia

Nicely rounded, sherbet-like fizz with unaggressive dryness and rich, vanilla-like fruit. Either drink as a great aperitif, or try a glass with fruit-based puddings.

SWEET SPARKLING WHITE

Asti Spumante, Somerfield

■ £4.79 ■ Italy

A tropical fruit salad aroma and rounded, yeasty, grapey, not too sweet flavours make this difficult to resist. As its aroma suggests, try it with fruit salad.

Moscato Fizz, Somerfield

■ £1.99 ■ Italy

Sweet, yet almost peppery aromas and floral, spicy flavours. A long, tangy aftertaste follows. Serve as an aperitif or try it with smoked salmon.

DRY ROSE

Vin de Pays des Coteaux de la Cabrerisse, Domaine de la Bouletière, 1992

■ £3.59 ■ France

Organically produced, the ripe cherry flavour of this dry, elegant rosé makes it taste as if it must be good for you. Goes well with white fish dishes.

SWEET ROSE

California Blush, Somerfield

■ £3.45 ■ USA

Perfumed, honeyed rosé with just a hint of pink and raspberry-like, sweet flavour. Drink with pudding.

Valencia Rosado, Somerfield

■ £2.49 ■ Spain

Produced inland from the city of Valencia on Spain's east coast, this wine has an attractive rose petal aroma and flavour, with floral sweetness and a mouthwatering tang on the finish. Good with lightly spicy dishes.

KWIKSAVE

★★★ STAR BUYS ★★★

Leziria, Vino de Mesa Branco

■ £2.29 ■ Portugal ■ Star White

Produced northeast of Lisbon this is the bargain white of this book. Lightly fizzy, it has an appley flavour with tangy, easy-drinking fruit. A great aperitif and the ideal party white.

Shiraz, Pelican Bay

■ £2.79 ■ Australia ■ Star Red

This must be one of this year's best buys. Soft, plummy wine with an overriding flavour of violets and a hint of cinnamon on the finish. Serve anytime to turn an ordinary meal into an occasion.

Wines by Style

LIGHT DRY WHITE

Bordeaux Blanc Cuvée VE, 1992

■ £2.49 ■ France

Soft, gluggable, great value party white. Mix half and half with soda water to make the perfect spritzer.

Comtesse de Lorancy, EC blend, Bauhaud

■ £2.29 ■ France

Spot this wine by looking for the label that looks like

an airline envelope. It's obviously a well travelled wine as the grapes come from Spain and France, and somewhere along the line it picked up its fancy title! Dry, pleasant, very cheap everyday drinking – great for parties and much better than many other EC blends.

Leziria, Vino de Mesa Branco

■ £2.29 ■ Portugal

Produced northeast of Lisbon this is the bargain white of this book. Lightly fizzy, it has an appley flavour with tangy, easy-drinking fruitiness. A great aperitif and the ideal party white.

Sauvignon Blanc, Bordeaux, Cuvée VE, 1992

■ £2.67 ■ France

Excellent value for money. You can't go wrong with this dry, quaffable, slightly medicinal white with a tang of gooseberries on the finish. An anytime wine.

Semillon-Chardonnay, Jacob's Creek, 1992

■ £3.89 ■ Australia

Widely available from many other stores, this is, deservedly, one of Britain's best selling whites. Lots of melon-like dry fruit flavours, with slightly cordial-like notes. Good with barbecued and smoked food.

Vin de Pays de l'Hérault Blanc, Cellier Maubertin, (1 litre), 1992

■ £2.99 ■ France

At the equivalent price of £2.24 for a normal-sized 75cl bottle, this crisp, refreshingly drinkable white is a real bargain.

MEDIUM-DRY WHITE

Bereich Nierstein, K Linden, 1991

■ £2.49 ■ Germany

A zippy, earthy white with off-dry fruit flavour and a crisp tang of lemony acidity on the finish. Try it with sardines.

Cape Medium White, Clearsprings, Simonsvlei

■ £2.69 ■ South Africa

Brilliant value for money. You can't go wrong with this easy-drinking, zippy, floral party white.

Hock, Deutscher Tafelwein, K Linden, 1992

■ £1.99 ■ Germany

This is a spicy, off-dry, lemony style white, with tangy, appley flavours. An anytime wine, ideal for party drinking.

Liebfive (5% alcohol)

■ £1.49 ■ Germany

Look for the handy screw-cap bottle. A light white with just 5% alcohol, towards the sweeter end of medium-dry. An appealing and affordable, gulpable wine.

Liebfraumilch, Peter Mertes

■ £1.97 ■ Germany

A zippy, sherbety wine; easy-drinking and excellent value for money. Serve anytime.

Morio-Muskat, Pfalz, 1992

■ £2.39 ■ Germany

Ignore the pastel label reminiscent of a box of tissues and concentrate on the luscious, tangy, grapey flavour. An earthy party wine. You can't go wrong at this price.

Piesporter Michelsberg, K Linden, 1992

■ £2.67 ■ Germany

Produced from vineyards surrounding the small village of Piesport on the banks of the Mosel, this has soft, honeyed aromas and light, flowery fruit character. A good aperitif.

FULL-BODIED DRY WHITE

Chardonnay Collection, Vin de Pays Haute Vallée de l'Aude, 1992

■ £3.37 ■ France

Produced from the sunny hillsides of Limoux (better known for its sparkling wine, Blanquette de Limoux), this wine has a crisp, grassy aroma and lots of dry, smoky, tangy fruit flavour. Attractive, complex and nicely balanced. Delicious with smoked meats or fish.

Semillon, Pelican Bay, Southeast Australia

■ £2.79 ■ Australia

Look for the stylish dark green label with a pelican on it. Exceptional value for money, tropical fruit salad wine with dry, moreish fruit. Serve with seafood or chicken and mushroom pie, mushroom risotto or with soup.

LIGHT RED

Cape Red, Clearsprings, Simonsvlei

■ £2.69 ■ South Africa

A fruity, easy-drinking red with soft, lightly spicy, rounded fruit flavour. Drink on its own or with soup, sandwiches or salad. Excellent value for money, this wine is cheaper here than at Asda.

Leziria Tinto

■ £2.29 ■ Portugal

This is brilliant value for money and even cheaper here than at Gateway or Budgens. Produced northeast of Lisbon it has an earthy, raspberry aroma and soft, creamy, raspberry flavour with a good tang of acidity. An anytime-drinking party red; can be drunk chilled.

Valpolicella, Cantine Sociale de Soave, 1992

■ £2.67 ■ Italy

Produced on the hillsides outside Verona, this is earthy, with attractive cherry flavours and lots of rough-and-ready spice. Good with herby, spicy pasta dishes.

MEDIUM-BODIED RED

Cabernet Sauvignon, Vin de Pays d'Oc, 1992

■ £2.59 ■ France

At this price, buy a case fast! Ripe, jammy aromas conjure up the heat of the south of France and are followed by simple, plummy flavour and a soft finish. Easy-drinking and excellent with anything cooked with olives, especially red meats.

Cabernet Sauvignon-Merlot, Lovico Suhindol

■ £2.29 ■ Bulgaria

This is a bargain you cannot afford to miss. Rough-and-ready fruitiness with a spicy finish. Serve with spaghetti and chilli.

Californian Premium Red, Maxfield Vineyards

■ £2.99 ■ USA

A cheap and cheerful, soft red with a touch of ripe grape sweetness. Great wine for parties which can be drunk chilled.

Côtes du Rhône, F Dubessy, 1992

■ £2.99 ■ France

Rustic, jammy red with lots of juicy, berry-like fruit flavour. Serve with strong, hard cheese or rabbit. Great value for money.

Merlot, Il Paesano

■ £2.29 ■ Italy

This wine is easy to recognize by its diagonal strip label. A soft, rounded, easy-drinking red with earthy fruit character. Brilliant value, ideal for parties.

Merlot, Vin de Pays d'Oc, Domaine Resclause, 1992

■ £2.85 ■ France

Produced between Béziers and Narbonne, this is a bargain southern French red. Jammy, with fully flavoured, rounded fruitiness, ideal with rich stews or beef in red wine.

Merlot & Pamid, Iambol, Vintage Blend, 1991

■ £2.49 ■ Bulgaria

A bargain wine with an arty label. Tangy and rounded with earthy, zippy fruit on the finish. Drink with steak and kidney pie or bangers and mash.

Valdepeñas, Ribera del Azur, Cencibel, Casa de la Viña, 1992

■ £2.49 ■ Spain

Attractive ripe blackberry aromas and flavours with a nice hint of sweetness. Very moreish, especially at this price. A great all-rounder to cheer up even the most ordinary of suppers.

Vin de Pays de l'Hérault Rouge, Cellier Maubertin, (1 litre), 1992

■ £2.99 ■ France

A soft, rounded, moreish wine with flavours of violets and spicy red berries. Serve with roast guinea-fowl, poussin or turkey. Brilliant value for money – the equivalent to £2.25 a bottle.

FULL-BODIED RED

Cabernet Sauvignon, Californian, Maxfield Vineyards, 1992

■ £3.39 ■ USA

With a full blackcurrant fruit flavour and ripe, roasted character, this is an excellent value, anytime-drinking red.

Cabernet Sauvignon-Shiraz, Butterfly Ridge, Angove's

■ £3.39 ■ Australia

The purple butterfly on the label signifies the abundance of butterflies that fly around in the Adelaide Foothills where this wine is made. Lots of powerful, ripe, currant-like rich fruit flavours make it the ideal complement to any dish in a red wine sauce.

Shiraz, Pelican Bay

■ £2.79 ■ Australia

This must be one of this year's bargains. Soft, plummy wine with an overriding flavour of violets and a hint of cinnamon on the finish. Serve anytime to turn an ordinary meal into an occasion.

SWEET WHITE

Moscatel de Valencia, Castillo de Liria

■ £2.99 ■ Spain

Enticing barley sugar aromas and rich, marmalade flavours make this a very moreish (and strong at 15% alcohol). The screw-top bottle means it is easy to keep in the fridge, where, once opened, it will last for two weeks without deteriorating (if you can resist drinking it). Delicious with creamy, fruity puddings.

DRY SPARKLING WHITE

Great Western Brut Reserve, Seppelt

■ £4.79 ■ Australia

Nicely rounded, sherbet-like fizz with unaggressive

dryness and rich, vanilla-like flavour. Either serve as an aperitif, or try it with fruit-based puddings.

SWEET SPARKLING WHITE

Lambrusco Bianco

■ £1.49 ■ Italy

Tangy, sweet, appley (5% alcohol) fizz. Once opened, the screw-cap will keep it fizzy for at least a week.

Lambrusco Bianco Riunite

■ £2.19 ■ Italy

This medium-sweet fizz is quite yeasty with lots of floral grape flavour. It's easy to drink lots of it when very chilled as it only has 7.5% alcohol.

SWEET SPARKLING ROSE

Lambrusco Rosé

■ £1.49 ■ Italy

Unusual floral, rose petal aromas and a very aromatic sweet fruit flavour with cinnamon-like spiciness. 5% alcohol. Serve with egg custard or *crème caramel.*

SPARKLING RED

Lambrusco Rosso Riunite

■ £2.29 ■ Italy

Fairly sweet but tangy red fizz with overtones of blackcurrants. Serve very chilled. Try it poured over vanilla ice-cream as an unusual ice-cream soda.

MARKS & SPENCER

★★★ STAR BUYS ★★★

Vin de Table Français, Jeunes Vignes, St-Michael

■ £4.99 ■ France ■ Star White

An old favourite, this wine seems expensive for a mere table wine until you taste its lightly toasted, creamy, dry fruit flavour. It is made from Chablis vines too young to make wine called Chablis, and actually tastes better than many 'proper' Chablis at twice the price. Serve it with soup, fish pâté, smoked salmon or salad. One of the best whites in this book.

Cabernet Sauvignon, Bulgarian, Svischtov Region, St-Michael, 1989

■ £2.99 ■ Bulgaria ■ Star Red

This wine jumps out of the glass and shouts 'blackberries, drink me!'. It has delicious rounded fruit flavour with a hint of grapey sweetness. Drink with game or steak and kidney pie.

Wines by Style

LIGHT DRY WHITE

Australian Dry White, Cotton Ridge, Angove's, St-Michael

■ £3.49 ■ Australia

Produced in the Murray Valley, this is made from a blend of different flowery, spicy grape varieties, so while the resulting wine is dry, it has lots of spicy fruit flavours too. Try serving it with lightly curried dishes.

Chardonnay, Premium Varietal, Stellenbosch, St-Michael, 1993

■ £3.99 ■ South Africa

Light and tangy with attractive buttery fruit flavours and a citrus taste on the finish. Well made and very easy to drink. An excellent complement to turkey, chicken or seafood pasta dishes.

Chardonnay, Vin de Pays d'Oc, Domaine Mandeville, St-Michael, 1993

■ £3.99 ■ France

One glance at the sunflowers on the label is enough to transport you down to southern France where this wine is produced from vineyards between Narbonne and Carcassonne. Ripe, soft and rounded, and full of classic Chardonnay characteristics, this is a versatile white, very easy to drink at anytime and with almost any dish.

Chardonnay-Semillon, Hunter Valley, Tyrells, St-Michael, 1992

■ £4.99 ■ Australia

A wine with rich, toasted aroma and lots of tropical fruit flavours. Serve it with roast turkey or bacon sandwiches.

Colombard, Cape Country, Breede River Valley, KWV, St-Michael, 1993

■ £3.29 ■ South Africa

Clean, crisp and tangy South African wine from the Colombard grape, with underlying floral, spicy flavours. Serve with lightly spiced dishes like garlic mushrooms or prawns.

Frascati Superiore, Pallavicini SAITA, St-Michael, 1993

■ £3.99 ■ Italy

Sold in a distinctive squat bottle, this has a citrus aroma and light, appley fruit flavour. Serve as an aperitif or with seafood.

Muscadet de Sèvre-et-Maine, Domaine des Balluettes, Ackerman-Laurence, St-Michael, 1992

■ £3.99 ■ France

An easy-drinking dry white wine with lots of mouth-watering fruity flavours. An anytime, or any occasion aperitif.

Vintages and Prices
Whilst every care has been taken to ensure that vintages and prices of wines detailed in *Check it Out* are the same as those on sale, it is possible that some will have changed. If a more recent vintage is in stock, the quality should be comparable, and therefore a similar buy. (With the majority of whites, especially light and medium-dry whites, a rule of thumb is 'the younger the vintage, the fresher the wine'.)

Sauvignon Blanc, Cape Country, Breede River Valley, KWV, St-Michael, 1993

■ £3.29 ■ South Africa

This is a rounded white, with appealing fruit flavour – nothing like as acidic as French Sauvignon Blancs can be. A value for money, anytime wine too. Try serving it as an excellent complement to any veal or chicken dish.

Soave, Girelli (1 litre), St-Michael

■ £3.99 ■ Italy

Moreish party wine with a handy screw-top bottle. Attractive, with soft, floral fruitiness and a zippy, fresh, citrus finish.

Vin de Pays des Côtes de Gascogne, Patrick Azcue, St-Michael, 1993

■ £2.99 ■ France

Lively, aromatic, with floral flavours and a tangy aftertaste – the kind of wine the Three Musketeers (local to this region) would have loved knocking back, if it had been around at the time!

Vin de Table Blanc, Sélection Blanc, Duboeuf, St-Michael

■ £2.99 ■ France

This flowery-labelled wine is made from an unusual combination of grapes from southern France and La Mancha in Spain, carefully blended by Beaujolais expert Georges Duboeuf. The result is a very drinkable, dry aperitif-style white.

Vin de Table Français, Jeunes Vignes, St-Michael

■ £4.99 ■ France

An old favourite, this wine seems expensive for a mere table wine until you taste its lightly toasted, creamy, dry fruit. It is made from Chablis vines too young to make wine called Chablis, and it actually tastes better than many 'proper' Chablis at twice the price. Serve with soup, fish pâté, smoked salmon or salad. One of the best whites in this book.

MEDIUM-DRY WHITE

Chenin Blanc, Cape Country, Coastal Region, KWV, St-Michael, 1992

■ £3.29 ■ South Africa

Crisp, easy-drinking, flowery white wine with a tangy fruit flavour. Very moreish. Try serving it with seafood.

Hock, Deutscher Tafelwein Rhein, Klosterhof (1 litre), St-Michael

■ £3.99 ■ Germany

Sold in a handy screw-top litre bottle. The wine inside has a grapey aroma and a flavour of spicy mince-pies. Drink as an aperitif or serve it with puddings and cakes.

Liebfraumilch, Klosterhof Rheinhessen, St-Michael

■ £2.99 (75 cl), £3.99 (litre) ■ Germany

Slightly drier than some, with an attractive floral fruit

flavour. Good with lightly spiced dishes like chicken with olives.

Medium White, Vin de Table, Plaimont (1 litre), St-Michael

■ £4.29 ■ France

A good value white French *vin de table*, with easy-drinking, medium-dry, flowery fruit flavours. An ideal party wine, on sale in an easily accessible, screw-top bottle.

Piesporter Michelsberg, Hegemann, St-Michael, 1993

■ £3.49 ■ Germany

Produced from a blend of Müller-Thurgau and Riesling grapes, this wine has refreshing fruit flavour and a crisp citrus tang on the finish. Serve with salads or fish and chips.

FULL-BODIED DRY WHITE

Chardonnay, Bin 65, Lindemans, St-Michael, 1993

■ £4.99 ■ Australia

An attractive creamy aroma and zippy floral fruit flavours, followed by a smoky, mouthwatering after-taste which makes you reach for another glass. Good with char-grilled or barbecued food.

Chardonnay, Gisborne, St-Michael, 1993

■ £4.99 ■ New Zealand

Produced on the east coast of New Zealand's North

Island, this has attractive cordial-like fruit flavour with good acidity on the finish. Serve with roast chicken.

LIGHT RED

Beaujolais, Cellier des Samsons, St-Michael, 1993

■ £3.99 ■ France

Light and jammy, with earthy, juicy, fruitiness. Serve with roast chicken or quail.

Beaujolais-Villages, Duboeuf, St-Michael, 1992

■ £4.99 ■ France

As the label says of this wine's producer, Georges Duboeuf, 'not for nothing is he known as the King of Beaujolais', and the wine, while not cheap, is well worth its price and reputation. It has lots of full-bodied juicy fruit flavours, with excellent, stylish balance. Drinkable at anytime, chilled or otherwise. Tastes especially good when served with baked ham or with spicy salami.

Gamay, Vin de Pays des Coteaux de l'Ardèche, St-Michael

■ £3.49 ■ France

The Beaujolais grape, Gamay, has been transplanted to the south of France where it takes on a more floral flavour along with its characteristic bubblegum nuances. This resulting *vin de pays* is juicy, fruity and easy-drinking. Great chilled, and a good wine for picnics or parties.

Vin de Table, Selection Rouge, Duboeuf, St-Michael

■ £3.29 ■ France

Tasty table wine from Georges Duboeuf, the 'King' of Beaujolais. It's easy-drinking, with lots of juicy, cherry fruit flavours and an earthy tang of acidity on the finish. A versatile wine, try it served chilled with a crispy bacon salad.

MEDIUM-BODIED RED

Cabernet Sauvignon, Bulgarian, Svischtov Region, St-Michael, 1989

■ £2.99 ■ Bulgaria

This wine's aroma jumps out of the glass and shouts 'blackberries, drink me!'. It has delicious rounded fruit flavours too, with a hint of grapey sweetness. A delicious complement to game dishes or steak and kidney pie.

Côtes du Roussillon-Villages, Full French Red, Vignerons Catalans (1 litre), St-Michael

■ £4.49 ■ France

Produced in the foothills of the Pyrenees, this is litre-bottle wine worth keeping in stock as everyone will like its soft, berry-like, plummy fruit flavours. A touch of liquorice on the finish adds even more to its character and makes it excellent value for money. Drink it on its own or serve it with duck, cassoulet or chilli. It's also a good one to remember for making mulled wine.

Merlot del Veneto, Vino de Tavola, Girelli, St-Michael

■ £2.99 ■ Italy

Unusual violet aromas, flavours of cherries and soft, ripe, Victoria plums, then a curranty aftertaste. Great with cheese on toast, pasta or steak sandwiches.

Montepulciano d'Abruzzo, Girelli, St-Michael, 1993

■ £2.99 ■ Italy

A rough-and-ready red with attractive cherry flavours. Serve with spicy pasta or pizza.

Vin de Pays de l'Hérault, Domaine St-Pierre, St-Michael, 1993

■ £3.49 ■ France

A perfumed wine with flavours of violets; easy-drinking, simple, drink anytime. Serve with pasta and pesto or mushroom omelettes.

Vino da Tavola, Italian Red, Girelli (1 litre), St-Michael

■ £3.99 ■ Italy

Handy screw-cap litre bottle of gluggable, rough-and-ready red. Ideal party or picnic wine.

FULL-BODIED RED

Cabernet Sauvignon, Bin 37, Orlando, St-Michael, 1991

■ £4.99 ■ Australia

A rich, chocolatey, minty smell followed by luscious, full, dry, berry-like fruit flavours. You could serve this with the grandest dinner.

Classic Claret, Château Lacousse, Bordeaux, St-Michael, 1993

■ £3.99 ■ France

Soft, tobacco-like nose; good dry fruit flavour with plenty of ripe, blackcurrant notes. Drink with roast poussin, guinea-fowl or chicken.

Fitou, Les Producteurs de Mont Tauch, St-Michael, 1991

■ £3.79 ■ France

This wine has a rich, meaty aroma and lots of fruit and vanilla on the palate. Ideal with any dish laced with herbs and garlic.

SWEET SPARKLING WHITE

Lambrusco White, Girelli, St-Michael

■ £1.99 (75cl), 2.49 (litre) ■ Italy

Easy-drinking, honeyed fizz, with light, hazelnut overtones. Try drinking it with chocolate pudding.

SWEET ROSE

Rosé d'Anjou, UAPL (1 litre), St-Michael

■ £4.79 ■ France

A handy screw-top litre bottle to keep in the fridge. Lots of marzipan-like aromas and cherry-like sweet, yet not cloying, fruitiness. Ideal for drinking anytime.

SWEET SPARKLING ROSE

Lambrusco Rosé, Girelli, St-Michael

■ £1.99 (75cl), £2.49 (1 litre) ■ Italy

Ignore the rather unattractive flesh-coloured label on this bottle – the wine actually tastes good! It's rather like alcoholic (5%) strawberry jam. Serve with strawberry or raspberry ripple ice-cream.

Vintages and Prices

Whilst every care has been taken to ensure that vintages and prices of wines detailed in *Check it Out* are the same as those on sale, it is possible that some will have changed. If a more recent vintage is in stock, the quality should be comparable, and therefore a similar buy. (With the majority of whites, especially light and medium-dry whites, a rule of thumb is 'the younger the vintage, the fresher the wine'.)

MORRISONS

★★★ STAR BUYS ★★★

Graves, (Oak Aged), Château Saint Gallier, 1992

■ £4.29 ■ France ■ Star White

Forget the old style Graves which was either cloying and sweet or dry and flabby. Today's new style wines are crisp and dry. This is a stunning, rich, oaky one with soft vanilla and rounded whitecurrant flavours. It tastes like a £7 bottle. Serve with trout and almonds, or chicken dishes.

Shiraz-Cabernet, Bin 35, Penfolds, 1992

■ £4.29 ■ Australia ■ Star Red

A really rich red with masses of black cherry flavoured fruit. An immensely powerful, flavourful wine which would go with the richest game.

Wines by Style

LIGHT DRY WHITE

Blossom Hill White, California

■ £3.39 ■ USA

An unusual, slightly minty aroma from this California wine combines with a light, melon-like flavour and spicy overtones. A delicious match for pasta and pesto sauce.

Bordeaux Blanc, 'La Taste', 1992

■ £2.69 ■ France

Aptly named, this is a wine you'll get 'a taste' for. Soft, with a slightly nutty aroma, it's crisp, dry and very moreish. Drink with seafood or charcuterie.

Chardonnay, Lutomer, 1991

■ £2.99 ■ Yugoslavia

From the makers of Laski Rizling. Tangy, floral, complex flavours for a wine of its price. Good for parties.

Est! Est!! Est!!!, Canaletto, 1992

■ £2.99 ■ Italy

A travelling Bishop in 1111 instructed his servant to go on ahead and mark inn doors with 'est' if they sold wine. Those with excellent wine were marked est! est!! est!!!, or so goes the story. This one has an attractive, honey aroma and dry, zippy flavour. Ideal with pasta.

Graves, (Oak Aged), Château Saint Gallier, 1992

■ £4.29 ■ France

Forget the old style Graves which was either cloying and sweet or dry and flabby. Today's new style is crisp and dry. This is stunning, rich and oaky with soft vanilla and rounded whitecurrant flavours. It tastes like a £7 bottle. Serve with trout and almonds, or chicken.

Graves Blanc, Ginestet, 1992

■ £3.69 ■ France

Light and zippy, this new-style Graves goes well with creamy fish dishes or scallops pan-fried with bacon.

Muscadet de Sèvre-et-Maine Sur Lie, La Sablière, Alban St-Pre, 1992

■ £3.49 ■ France

Dry, refreshing, with good acidity tempered with a light, creamy, yeasty flavour. Serve with pan-fried or creamy scallops.

Pinot Blanc, Preiss-Zimmer, 1992

■ £3.99 ■ France

This is a light, elegantly floral, well-balanced white made from the least spicy Alsace grape. Serve as an aperitif or with lightly smoked or spiced dishes.

Servus, Burgenland, 1992

■ £2.95 ■ Austria

Produced from grapes grown east of Vienna, this has a tangy, spicy fruit flavour. If you've yet to try an Austrian wine this is a good one to start with. Goes well with stir-fried spicy prawns or chicken.

Trebbiano Vigneti del Sole, Pasqua, 1992

■ £2.49 ■ Italy

Keep a few bottles of this in the fridge for unexpected guests – it's incredibly versatile. Lots of rounded fruit flavours with a dry, zippy, lemony aftertaste. Great with all kinds of chicken dishes.

Vin de Pays des Côtes de Gascogne, Pouy, Domaines Grassa, 1992

■ £2.99 ■ France

The region's top producer comes up trumps with this

wine: it has unusual violet, chocolatey overtones, the sort usually found in red wine. Interested? Then try it!

Vino de la Tierra del Valle de Monterrey, Domino Blanco

■ £2.49 ■ Spain

Produced in Galicia in northwest Spain, this is an easy-drinking, anytime wine with pleasant, dry, rounded fruit flavour. Great for picnics and parties, especially at this bargain price.

MEDIUM-DRY WHITE

Côtes de Bergerac Moelleux, Foncaussad, 1992

■ £3.29 ■ France

A flowery white with flavours of marmalade. Soft, rounded, easy-drinking. Serve with blue cheese, roast chicken or duck.

Flonheimer Adelberg Kabinett, Rheinhessen, J Egberts, 1991

■ £2.59 ■ Germany

Perfumed, honeyed white with zippy, moreish fruit flavour. A great wine for picnics.

Vintages and Prices

Whilst every care has been taken to ensure that vintages and prices of wines detailed in *Check it Out* are the same as those on sale, it is possible that some will have changed. If a more recent vintage is in stock, the quality should be comparable, and therefore a similar buy. (With the majority of whites, especially light and medium-dry whites, a rule of thumb is 'the younger the vintage, the fresher the wine'.)

Gabbia d'Oro Bianco

■ £2.19 ■ Italy

Look for the diagonal strip label complete with coat of arms. A fruity, slightly honeyed table wine with lots of soft, rounded flavour. Good for parties.

Nussdorfer Bischopskreuz Auslese, Weinkellerei am Klostergarten, Pfalz, 1992

■ £3.55 ■ Germany

Lemon and honey aroma with lemony, barley flavour. Serve with lemon meringue pie or soft blue cheese.

Ortega Spätlese, St-Johanner Abtey, Rheinhessen, 1992

■ £2.99 ■ Germany

An unusual aroma of parma violet sweets and floral fruit flavours with a limey flavoured tang. Great with Thai food with lemon grass and lime leaves.

Wehlener Klosterberg Kabinett, Mosel, 1991

■ £3.59 ■ Germany

An earthy, zippy wine with off-dry, tangy fruit flavours. Ideal with fruit salads or chicken or duck with a fruit sauce.

FULL-BODIED DRY WHITE

Chardonnay, Bin 65, Lindemans, 1993

■ £4.69 ■ Australia

An attractive creamy aroma with zippy, floral fruit flavour... then a smoky, mouthwatering aftertaste which makes you reach for another glass. Good with char-grilled or barbecued food.

Chardonnay, Proprietor's Reserve, Glen Ellen, 1991

■ £3.99 ■ USA

A tropical fruit smell and flavour make this wine hard to resist. Tangy citrus acidity mixed with a touch of honey on the finish means it's the ideal foil for guinea-fowl, poussin or crispy Peking duck served with plum sauce.

Fumé Blanc, L A Cetto, 1992

■ £3.99 ■ Mexico

Crisp, green, gooseberry aromas and lots of flinty, slightly flowery, dry fruitiness. Nobody would guess it came from Mexico. Drink as a stylish aperitif or with smoked salmon.

Sauvignon Blanc, Gisborne, Cooks, 1992

■ £4.79 ■ New Zealand

Green, grassy aromas with a hint of basil, and crisp, dry, limey fruit flavour. Serve with smoked haddock, roast chicken or wokked prawns.

Semillon-Chardonnay, Coldridge Estates, Southeast Australia

■ £3.29 ■ Australia

The stylish triangle-shaped label depicts an Australian native plant, the 'yellow gum'. An unusual wine which smells like marmalade and has a herbal, peachy flavour. Goes well with sweet-and-sour dishes.

LIGHT RED

Beaujolais, Champclos, 1992

■ £3.29 ■ France

Unusually perfumed with earthy, raspberry flavours and an attractive peppery, tangy finish. Great with strong garlicky meats like Toulouse sausage.

Beaujolais-Villages, Leger, 1992

■ £3.79 ■ France

A big, rounded, earthy, fruity Beaujolais with lots of mouthwatering acidity on the finish. Serve with chilli con carne, cassoulet or red mullet.

Gabbia d'Oro Rosso

■ £2.19 ■ Italy

Easy to recognize by its distinctive diagonal strip label. Lots of rounded, soft, plummy fruit flavours and nice balancing acidity. A great party wine – a good all-rounder which can be drunk chilled.

Gamay de Touraine, Guerois, 1992

■ £2.69 ■ France

Gamay is the Beaujolais grape, but grown in the Loire Valley to make this wine. Lots of earthy, jammy fruit is balanced by tangy, zippy acidity. Fairly rough-and-ready, ideal with coarse pâté.

Vin du Pays du Jardin de la France, St-Arnould, 1992

■ £2.49 ■ France

Maybe the flowers on this label refer to the name of the Loire Valley region – 'jardin' translates to garden – but they could equally describe the wine, which has a floral, highly perfumed aroma, backed up by juicy fruit flavour and a refreshing tang of acidity. Serve with *coq au vin*.

MEDIUM-BODIED RED

Blossom Hill, California

■ £3.39 ■ USA

Spot this wine by looking for the flowery label. An easy-drinking red which smells and tastes like fruitcake. Serve with peppered steak or beef curry.

Bordeaux Rouge, Ginestet

■ £2.89 ■ France

A bargain claret, with masses of straightforward, curranty flavour. At this price, buy a few bottles for keeping for a year or two. Serve with roast beef or lamb.

Buzet, Renaissance, 1991

■ £3.59 ■ France

At £3.59 you cannot go wrong with this aptly named wine (sounds like 'boozy'!). Its ripe, firm, blackcurrant flavour makes it the ideal partner for roast duck, goose or red meats.

Cabernet Sauvignon, Hungary, 1991

■ £2.69 ■ Hungary

A wonderful whiff of ripe blackcurrants and a lightly peppery flavour. An easy-drinking, anytime wine.

Cabernet Sauvignon, Vin de Pays des Coteaux de l'Ardèche, Vignerons Ardèchois, 1992

■ £2.89 ■ France

A bargain red with masses of quite full-bodied, austere, spicy fruit flavour. Soften the tannin by decanting the wine. Serve with herby pizzas, pasta and pesto, or lamb with rosemary.

Corbières, les Fenouillets, 1992

■ £2.49 ■ France

This southern French red was made to go with wine-based Provençal-style stews or daubes, full of olives and herbs. Its violet flavours combine with rich, spiciness. Tastes like a wine costing twice its price.

Côtes de Bourg, Château Tour Camillac, 1989

■ £4.99 ■ France

This region to the north of Bordeaux produces excellent quality claret, generally with lots of ripe, plummy flavour and masses of body and style. This wine has enough fruitiness to cope with Peking-style duck with plum sauce.

Côtes de Frontonnais, 'Fronton', 1992

■ £3.99 ■ France

This attractive flowery painted bottle is easy to spot on the shelf. The wine is distinctive too, with masses of violet-like and herbal flavours on the palate. Delicious served with spicy pizza or tomato-based pasta dishes.

Côtes du Rhône-Villages, Epitalon

■ £3.29 ■ France

Rich, aromatic, spicy aroma and lots of plummy, spicy fruit flavour. This is what Côtes du Rhône should taste like though, sadly, few do. Serve with chicken roasted with garlic or beef stew.

Côtes du Roussillon-Villages, Le Millennaire, 1991

■ £2.79 ■ France

A spicy, plummy southern red with masses of moreish curranty fruit on the palate. Excellent value for money. Serve with rabbit, lamb or strong blue cheese.

Crozes-Hermitage, Cave de Tain l'Hermitage, 1990

■ £4.99 ■ France

Made near the village of Tain l'Hermitage, this wine is powerful, with an intense tarry, spicy aroma and ripe, spicy, quite tannic flavour. Serve with fully flavoured *coq au vin*, beef in red wine and olives or roast duck.

Fitou, Narbonne, 1990

■ £3.15 ■ France

A fairly safe bet from the Languedoc-Roussillon region with ripe, plummy fruit flavour and a spicy, earthy finish. Great with bangers and mash.

Médoc 'La Taste'

■ £3.69 ■ France

This wine's name is apt – you soon get a 'taste' for it.

Its aroma shouts blackcurrant and there's masses of moreish, similarly flavoured fruit to follow. Serve with beef and Guinness pie, barbecued and grilled steak.

Merlot, Romanian Reserve, Dealul Mare Region, 1987

■ £3.49 ■ Romania

If you've yet to try a Romanian red, this is an ideal one to start with. Its ripe, soft, oaky fruit flavour reminds me of rich, red Bordeaux. Serve with roast lamb or duck.

Merlot, Stambolovo Reserve, Haskovo Region, 1987

■ £3.49 ■ Bulgaria

A seductive aroma, like an old mature claret, with soft, rounded fruit flavour and a balancing tang of acidity on the finish. Try it with duck or goose.

Merlot, Vin de Pays d'Oc, Chantovent, 1992

■ £2.65 ■ France

Attractive, warm, raisiny, chocolatey aromas give way to highly perfumed violet fruit flavours and a touch of tannin on the finish – all with an overriding soft, velvetiness. Great with lamb roasted with rosemary.

Montepulciano d'Abruzzo, Cortenova, 1992

■ £2.75 ■ Italy

A ripe, plummy wine with yeasty overtones and rounded flavours, finishing with a hint of black cherries and a touch of ripe, sweet grapiness. Serve with roast lamb or pork.

Rioja Tinto, Bodegas Navajas, Morrisons, 1992

■ £2.99 ■ Spain

Light, floral aroma and flavour, with a good citrusy tangy aftertaste. Masses of fruit, the ideal foil for chicken with lots of garlic. Could be drunk chilled.

Sangredetoro, Torres, 1990

■ £3.99 ■ Spain

This bottle is made easily distinguishable by the plastic bull around its neck. An earthy, spicy, smoky red. Serve with pâté, game or wine-rich casseroles.

Vinho de Mesa, Soveral

■ £2.09 ■ Portugal

A powerfully flavoured wine with an attractive cherry aroma and flavour and masses of fruitiness. Drink with rich beef stew or steak and kidney pie.

FULL-BODIED RED

Abadia, Costers del Segre, Raimat, 1989

■ £4.99 ■ Spain

Serve this wine blind to your friends and they'll think they are drinking a £10 bottle! It has an enticing aroma of vanilla and cassis with a flavour like blackcurrant ice-cream, ripe with a hint of sweetness but still dry on the finish. Could cope with any strong food, especially game.

Cabernet Sauvignon, Bin 45, Lindemans, 1990

■ £4.69 ■ Australia

Roasted, berry-like aroma and lots of stylish concentrated blackcurrant flavour; rather bitter on the finish. Decanting softens the taste. Great with barbecued food.

Cabernet Sauvignon, L A Cetto, 1987

■ £3.99 ■ Mexico

If you've yet to taste a Mexican wine, this is the one to start with. It is rich and heavy, with a roasted, liquorice aroma and masses of lightly medicinal blackcurrant nuances mixed with vanilla. Tastes even better when decanted as this softens out the bitter flavours. Ideal with spicy Mexican food.

Cabernet Sauvignon, Sebastiani

■ £3.99 ■ USA

A very intense aroma is followed by even more vibrant blackcurrant flavour and smoky, berry-like overtones. Wonderful with char-grilled or barbecued meats.

Cabernet Sauvignon, Villa Montes, 1990

■ £3.99 ■ Chile

Very full-bodied and smoky with masses of earthy, curranty fruit flavour and fresh tobacco notes. Ideal with steak and kidney pie.

Malbec, Oak Cask Reserve, Trapiche, Mendoza, 1988

■ £4.29 ■ Argentina

Produced at the base of majestic snow-capped mountains, this is an exceptional wine. It has roasted fruit and vanilla aromas, with full-bodied blackcurrant and cream on the palate. The structure and oaky tannin mean this wine could be kept for a few years. It would taste even better after decanting.

Mavrodaphne of Patras (Sweet)

■ £3.49 ■ Greece

This oak-aged, sweet Greek red is definitely an acquired taste – you'll either love it or hate it! It smells like alcoholic marzipan and tastes like sweet, alcoholic currants. It's strong (15% alcohol), so a bottle is enough for 12 people if served in small glasses. Drink chilled with pâté, spicy soup, pudding or strong, hard cheese.

Shiraz-Cabernet, Bin 35, Penfolds, 1992

■ £4.29 ■ Australia

A really rich red with masses of black cherry flavoured fruit. An immensely powerful, flavourful wine which would go with the richest game.

DRY SPARKLING WHITE

Great Western Brut Reserve, Seppelt

■ £4.99 ■ Australia

Nicely rounded, sherbet-like fizz, with unaggressive dryness and rich, vanilla-like flavour. Drink as a great aperitif, or try a glass with fruit-based puddings.

SWEET SPARKLING WHITE

Asti Spumante, Gianni

■ £4.59 ■ Italy

Grapey aromas and a soft, appley finish make this fizz very moreish. Remember to serve it well chilled.

Moscato Spumante, Gianni

■ £3.39 ■ Italy

This wine has more body than many of its type, partly due to the higher alcohol level of 6.5%. It has a rich aroma of tangerines and honeyed lychee flavours on the palate. The pop of the cork adds to the sense of occasion.

DRY ROSE

Campanas Rosé, Navarra, 1992

■ £2.99 ■ Spain

Easy-drinking, dry and spicy rosé, this is the favourite pre-dinner (or lunch) tipple in the bars of Navarra, Rioja's lesser known, and therefore better value, neighbour.

Clairet Rosé

■ £3.49 ■ France

You can easily recognize this dark Bordeaux rosé (made by the same producer as Sainsbury's Clairet) by its distinctive label, complete with leggy green frog in a top hat holding a glass of it. He seems to be enjoying the wine's soft, rounded and dry, yet tangy fruit flavour!

Côtes de Provence Rosé

■ £2.99 ■ France

Bottled in an unusual pear-shaped bottle, this southern French rosé is quite full-bodied with ripe, earthy fruit flavour and a hint of spice. It's the ideal complement to garlicky dishes.

Vin de Pays des Pyrénées-Orientales, Rosé, le Vigneron Catalan

■ £2.49 ■ France

There are lovely fresh, grapey flavours in this full-bodied wine, conjuring up days of southern French sun. Its depth of flavour makes it a good partner to fairly fully flavoured dishes, even curry. Excellent value for money.

SWEET ROSE

White Zinfandel, Sebastiani

■ £3.49 ■ USA

A strange, sherbet-like wine which is pink (despite its name) and has a delicious tangy, strawberry sweetness on the finish. Great with any meat or fish dish which includes a fruit-based sauce.

SAFEWAY

★★★ STAR BUYS ★★★

Entre-Deux-Mers, Château Canet, (Organic), 1992

■ £3.99 ■ France ■ Star White

This is produced to the east of Bordeaux from Sémillon and Sauvignon Blanc grapes which have been grown without the use of chemical fertilisers or pesticides, and as a result should be better for you! It tastes so good it will confound the 'anti-green brigade'. Dry and rounded, this is well-crafted wine, ideal for everyday drinking.

Valdepeñas, Cencibel, Casa de la Viña, 1992

■ £3.29 ■ Spain ■ Star Red

A big, impressive wine which smells and tastes of ripe black cherries with a hint of bitter-sweet fruit on the finish. It tastes as if it should cost twice the price. Serve with game pie.

Wines by Style

LIGHT DRY WHITE

Australian Dry White, (Tetrapack), Safeway

■ £2.95 ■ Australia

Packaged in what looks like an orange-juice carton, the same size as a bottle but lighter to take on picnics. This is a dry, yeasty white with a lightly spicy tang.

Bianco di Custoza, 'I Frari', Santi

■ £3.75 ■ Italy

To find this wine on the shelf, simply look for the unusually tall, square-shouldered bottle. Produced from vines grown in the Lake Garda region, this is dry and zippy with lots of appley flavour. Serve with roast chicken or creamy fish and pasta dishes.

Blanc de Bordeaux, (Aged in Oak), Safeway, 1992

■ £3.99 ■ France

Produced from vineyards between the Garonne and Dordogne rivers, this is definitely a food wine. Its attractive oaky yet light, fresh aromas and dry vanilla fruit flavour make it ideal to drink with creamy chicken dishes.

Chardonnay, Gyöngyös Estate Hugh Ryman, 1992

■ £3.35 ■ Hungary

Pronounced 'join-josh', this comes from the town of the same name, northeast of Budapest. If you've yet to try a Hungarian wine this is a good one to start with. It has a rich, buttery aroma and lots of tropical fruit flavours, then a hint of sweetness on the finish. Drink with fish pâté, or lightly curried dishes.

Chardonnay, Kiskoros Region, Safeway, 1992

■ £2.99 ■ Hungary

A light wine, soft and easy-drinking, with pleasant flinty fruit flavours. At this price it's a wine you can serve anytime.

Chardonnay, Vino da Tavola del Triveneto, Safeway, 1992

■ £3.49 ■ Italy

Soft, appley flavour and a zippy lemon tang on the finish make this the ideal complement to lightly spiced chicken dishes or garlic prawns.

Chardonnay del Piemonte, 'Le Monferrine', 1992

■ £3.75 ■ Italy

Produced in the south of northern Italy's Piedmont region, this white has fresh fruit character with light, floral, almost violet nuances. The aftertaste of white-currants adds a refreshing tang to the finish. An ideal wine to serve with shellfish, especially creamy scallops.

Dry Muscat, Carmel Vineyards, Samson Region (Kosher), 1992

■ £3.15 ■ Israel

If you've yet to try an Israeli wine, this is a good one to start with. A sweet, grapey aroma gives the impression that it is an off-dry white, yet on the palate it is dry and spicy with violet overtones. Good with Chinese food.

Dry Muscat, Nagyrede, Safeway, 1992

■ £2.99 ■ Hungary

Flowery, spicy aromas make you think you are going to taste a sweet wine. However, on the palate the wine is floral and dry. Excellent with Chinese or spicy Thai dishes.

Dry White Wine, Taurau Valley, Gisborne, 1993

■ £3.99 ■ New Zealand

Honeyed, dry, great all-rounder white with a lightly nutty finish. A good aperitif, or with seafood or fish.

Entre-Deux-Mers, Château Canet, (Organic), 1992

■ £3.99 ■ France

This is produced to the east of Bordeaux from Sémillon and Sauvignon Blanc grapes grown without the use of chemical fertilisers or pesticides, and as a result should be better for you! It tastes so good it will confound the 'anti-green brigade'. Dry and rounded, this is well-crafted wine, ideal for everyday drinking.

French Colombard, Gallo

■ £3.49 ■ USA

Spicy and floral with a hint of apples and cinnamon, this wine would taste equally good with savoury dishes as it would with sweet ones.

Gaillac, Cave de Labastide de Levis, 1993

■ £3.65 ■ France

Peachy, pineapple flavoured, and dry, with a tropical aftertaste. Ideal if you usually find dry white too acidic. Good with duck and orange or lemon chicken.

Gewurztraminer, Vignerons à Turckheim, 1992

■ £4.99 ■ France

Lightly smoky aroma, with a light, dry, spicy flavour. An elegant, complex wine, not as overpowering as some tropical fruit flavoured Gewürztraminers can be. Serve with smoked salmon.

La Mancha, Safeway, 1992

■ £2.85 ■ Spain

Produced in central Spain, this is an easy-drinking, flowery dry white with a tangy aftertaste. Delicious with prawns cooked in sherry.

Leziria, Vino de Mesa Branco

■ £2.59 ■ Portugal

From northeast of Lisbon, this is the *Check it Out* bargain white. Lightly fizzy, it has an appley flavour with tangy, easy-drinking fruitiness. A great aperitif and the ideal party white. Much cheaper at KwikSave.

Mâcon-Villages, Caves de Viré, 1992

■ £4.99 ■ France

Soft, rounded flavour with lots of rich, mouthwatering, dry fruit. Goes well with Dover sole, plaice and smoked fish dishes like kedgeree.

Muscadet de Sèvre-et-Maine, Jean Beauquin, Safeway, 1992

■ £2.99 ■ France

Easy-drinking dry white, ideal as an aperitif. Serve with prawns, clams or mussels.

Muscadet de Sèvre-et-Maine Sur Lie, Château de la Botinière, 1992

■ £4.39 ■ France

Nicely balanced lemony, dry fruit and honey-like richness. Good with white river fish like pike and perch.

Pinot Blanc d'Alsace, Vignerons à Turckheim, 1992

■ £4.35 ■ France

A crisp, light, sherbety wine, with an attractive spicy aftertaste. The ideal complement to fondues, wokked prawns or fish pâté.

Ribatejo, Terre de Lobos, Vinho Regional, 1992

■ £3.19 ■ Portugal

Ripe, fruity aromas followed by tangy sherbet flavour. An unusual wine which would go well with dishes in creamy sauces.

Sauvignon, Bergerac, Safeway, 1992

■ £3.49 ■ France

You've heard of the detective, so now try the wine – which has no connection except its name! Dry and tangy, with a taste of Granny Smith apples. Try serving it with fish pâté.

Sauvignon Blanc, Vredendal, Olifants River, Co-op, 1993

■ £3.29 ■ South Africa

This wine has an unusual aroma of green grass and tropical fruits, followed by lots of green apple flavours on the palate with an earthy, tangy finish. Good with salad as it is pungent enough to cope with salad dressing.

Semillon-Chardonnay, Barossa Winery, Safeway, 1992

■ £3.79 ■ Australia

Rounded, easy-drinking white with soft, whitecurrant-like flavours. Slight touch of sweetness. Serve with smoked salmon and chicken.

Semillon-Chardonnay, Jacob's Creek, 1993

■ £3.99 ■ Australia

This is, deservedly, one of Britain's best selling whites. Lots of melon-like dry fruit and slightly cordial-like notes. Good with barbecued and smoked food.

Sicilian Dry White, Safeway

■ £2.99 ■ Italy

Masses of fruit flavour and a touch of spritz make this an excellent all-rounder. Medium-bodied rather than light, it's quite luscious too. Serve with chicken.

Stanlake, Thames Valley Vineyards, Safeway, 1992

■ £3.99 ■ England

Lively, zippy, tangy and very drinkable. Fresh as an English summer's day. Drink as an aperitif or mix with soda water to make a spritzer.

Traminer-Ezerjó, Hungarian Country Wine, Mór, 1992

■ £2.79 ■ Hungary

Spot this wine on the shelf by its simple handwritten label. Attractive aromatic wine, soft and honeyed and delicious with any sweet-and-sour dish. Rather like a mini Alsace Gewurztraminer but at a much cheaper price!

Valencia, (Oak Aged), Safeway, 1991

■ £2.99 ■ Spain

Produced on the east coast of Spain, this wine has an enticing aroma of vanilla essence with lots of smoky, oaky fruit flavour on the palate. Tastes delicious with a bacon sandwich or any smoked meat.

Vin de Pays des Côtes de Gascogne, La Coume de Peyre, 1993

■ £3.35 ■ France

Floral, melon-like flavour, with an attractive lemony tanginess on the finish. Very moreish. Try with lemon chicken or chicken tikka.

Vin de Pays d'Oc Sur Lie, Vignerons de Marseille, 1992

■ £3.35 ■ France

Produced from the vineyards between Béziers and Narbonne, this wine has lots of zippy fruit flavour and a melony aftertaste. Try a glass with mild to medium cheese, or chilled as an aperitif.

Vin de Pays du Vaucluse, Cellier de Marennon, Safeway, 1992

■ £2.85 ■ France

A soft, easy-drinking, appley white produced from vineyards around the mouth of the Rhône Valley. Try it with light vegetarian dishes.

MEDIUM-DRY WHITE

Bordeaux Blanc Demi-Sec, Safeway, 1992

■ £3.35 ■ France

Rounded, creamy, sherbet-like. Ideal with fish pâté.

Gewürztraminer Halbtrocken, Pfalz, Safeway

■ £4.45 ■ Germany

Look for the French-style wine bottle, the shape you'd normally see burgundy in. An intense aroma of tropical fruits, masses of marmalade flavour, and a hint of citrus on the finish. Serve with fish soup or pâté or fruit salad.

Liebfraumilch, Safeway, 1992

■ £2.39 ■ Germany

Attractive honeysuckle aroma, with soft, flowery fruit flavour. Serve with chicken or duck with orange.

Ruppertsberger Nussbien Riesling Kabinett, Rheinpfalz, 1990

■ £3.89 ■ Germany

Rich, honeyed aromas with moreish *crème caramel* flavour. A delicious aperitif or drink with smoked salmon.

Vinho Verde, Safeway

■ £3.19 ■ Portugal

Look for the dumpy bottle, easy to recognize on the shelf. Lightly fizzy white with crisp, refreshing fruit flavour, like Granny Smith apples. Good to drink as an aperitif, or with Chinese dishes.

FULL-BODIED DRY WHITE

Bourgogne Blanc, (Oak Aged), Safeway

■ £4.99 ■ France

Complex, buttery burgundy with elegant, whitecurrant flavour. Ideal with creamy chicken or coconut curry.

Chardonnay, Montana, Marlborough, 1992

■ £4.99 ■ New Zealand

Attractive buttery aromas are followed by rich, luscious fruit to the taste. A very moreish wine from New Zealand's largest exporter. Serve with barbecued meat, roast chicken or turkey.

Chardonnay, Riverina Wines, New South Wales, 1993

■ £3.99 ■ Australia

Crisp and zippy, with smoky-bacon overtones. Good as an aperitif or with a bacon sandwich.

Chardonnay, Rosemount Estate, Hunter Valley, 1993

■ £4.99 ■ Australia

Look for the diamond shaped label. Heavily toasted, creamy aromas with a roasted, exotic, peachy flavour. Delicious with crispy duck.

LIGHT RED

Australian Dry Red, (Tetrapak), Safeway

■ £2.95 ■ Australia

Don't worry that this looks like an orange juice carton, the wine tastes great. It's an easy-drinking, fairly rough-and-ready light red with a spicy finish. Serve with Chinese food.

Merlot, Russe Region, (Young Vatted), 1993

■ £2.85 ■ Bulgaria

An intense aroma of fruit-cake carries through onto the palate and with an added touch of plummy spiciness makes this very easy to drink. It's light, in that it doesn't have much bitter tannin, and certainly does not lack flavour. Try a glass with chilli con carne.

Merlot-Pinot Noir, Bulgarian Country Wine, Sliven

■ £2.69 ■ Bulgaria

Attractive chocolate and plum aromas with lightly spiced, plummy flavour. Easy-drinking, great value anytime wine. Makes cheese on toast far more exciting.

Ribatejo, Vinho de Mesa, Safeway

■ £2.89 ■ Portugal

Rough-and-ready red with earthy, cough mixture-like fruit flavour and a touch of cloves on the finish. Drink with strong, hard cheese.

Shiraz-Cabernet, Hardy's Stamp Series, 1992

■ £3.65 ■ Australia

Look for the label with the kangaroo stamp on it. Lots of rich, berry-like flavour and an earthy tang makes this wine very drinkable. Almost medium-bodied. Drink as an aperitif or with roast lamb or pork.

Vin de Pays de l'Ardèche, Safeway

■ £2.75 ■ France

Pleasantly light and fruity southern French red with spicy overtones. Serve chilled, great with picnics.

MEDIUM-BODIED RED

Bergerac, Safeway, 1992

■ £3.29 ■ France

Nothing to do with the Jersey detective of the same name, but worth getting to know. Similar to claret, and made from the same grapes (Cabernet Sauvignon and Merlot), this has lots of earthy fruit flavour with a liquorice finish. Serve with stews and casseroles.

Bordeaux, Château Castera, 1991

■ £3.99 ■ France

Soft, attractive, violet-like, red fruit flavour. Lots of velvety, chocolate flavour too and a good balance of curranty richness and tannin. Serve with rich, full flavoured meat dishes and chocolate mousse.

Chianti, Safeway, 1992

■ £3.35 ■ Italy

Lots of peppery fruitiness with cherry-like, earthy, rustic notes. Ideal with spicy dishes, even curry.

Claret, Bordeaux, (Oak Aged), Safeway, 1990

■ £4.69 ■ France

Only buy this if you like the flavour of oak, which is quite prominent in this wine. It does, however, have more than enough blackcurrant character to be well balanced. Serve with char-grilled meat.

Coteaux du Languedoc, Domaine Grange du Pin, 1992

■ £3.59 ■ France

Ripe, fruity aroma and lots of earthy, rounded red fruit flavour on the palate, then finishing off with creamy blackcurrant notes on the finish. Great with beef and Guinness pie, peppered steak or steak and kidney pie.

Côtes du Rhône, Château Joanny, 1992

■ £3.99 ■ France

On the label of this wine we are treated to a balding mug-shot of Joanny Dupond (who he?) after whom the wine is named. This is a Côtes du Rhône with lots of stylish, peppery, rounded violet flavour and earthy, spicy overtones. Serve with roast lamb, beef cooked with red wine and garlic or *coq au vin.*

Côtes du Roussillon-Villages, Vignerons Catalans, Safeway

■ £3.29 ■ France

Jammy, with an attractive, almost floral aroma, this has lots of delicious, sun-drenched spicy fruit flavour. Serve with pheasant, guinea-fowl or pigeon.

Dry Reserve, E & J Gallo

■ £3.69 ■ USA

Earthy and tarry, with flavours of ripe blackcurrants. Drink with beef and olives or steak and kidney pie.

Montepulciano d'Abruzzo, Cantina Miglianico, 1992

■ £3.25 ■ Italy

Rich, almost beefy aroma and ripe, earthy, fruitiness. Serve with char-grilled steak or barbecued meat.

Saint Emilion, Gabriel Corcol, 1990

■ £4.99 ■ France

Many wines bearing this famous name are not worth the money. This one is, however: an aroma of spicy, plummy fruit is followed by thick, rich, velvety flavour. Serve with roast beef, or beef and Guinness pie.

Sicilian Red, Vino da Tavola, Safeway

■ £2.99 ■ Italy

The aroma of raspberries and cream makes this wine hard to resist. With rich, velvety fruit on the palate, it tastes like a wine costing twice its price. Serve anytime.

Valdepeñas, Bodegas Felix Solis, (Oak Aged), Safeway, 1988

■ £3.39 ■ Spain

Rich, vanilla aromas with lots of lightly minty blackcurrant fruit flavour and a hint of sweet tobacco. Serve with lamb chops and mint sauce.

Valdepeñas, Cencibel, Casa de la Viña, 1992

■ £3.29 ■ Spain

A big, impressive wine which smells and tastes of ripe black cherries, finishing with a hint of bitter-sweet fruit. Tastes as if it cost twice the price. Serve with game pie.

Vino da Tavola di Sicilia, Don Giovanni, 1991

■ £3.55 ■ Italy

A stylish wine, with an attractive mixture of cherry stone and soft, rounded, oaky flavours, then a touch of sweetness on the finish. Serve with rabbit or pigeon.

FULL-BODIED RED

Cabernet Sauvignon Reserve, Sliven, 1987

■ £3.29 ■ Bulgaria

Straightforward blackcurrant flavours and earthiness reminiscent of an austere claret. The touch of oak on the finish makes it a wine ideal with smoked meats.

Cabernet Sauvignon, Nottage Hill, Hardy's, 1991

■ £4.25 ■ Australia

Beefy, minty red with lots of mouth-filling fruit. The perfect foil for anything meaty like beef and onion pie, hefty beefburgers with relish, or a hot, fiery chilli.

Cabernet Sauvignon, Orlando RF, 1991

■ £4.99 ■ Australia

This easy-drinking, fruity red has lots of flavour, balanced by structure and power. Good with blue cheese.

Cabernet Sauvignon, Riverina Wines, New South Wales, 1992

■ £3.89 ■ Australia

This is on the lighter side of full-bodied, high in juicy, plummy flavour, but low in tannin. As a result it is alarmingly easy to drink. Good with cold meats, especially spicy salamis.

Copertino, Cantina Sociale Coop Copertino, 1989

■ £3.59 ■ Italy

Produced in the heel of Italy, this wine has peppery fruit flavour and a cherry aroma. Excellent value for money. Great with beef in red wine.

Corbières, Château de Caraguilhes, (Organic), Safeway, 1990

■ £4.39 ■ France

Look for the attractive painted bottle which looks as good as this wine tastes. This is Corbières with a rich, tarry aroma, masses of full-bodied, plummy flavour and quite a tannic, powerful finish. Delicious served with game.

Salice Salentino Riserva, Cosimo Taurino, Apulia, 1988

■ £4.59 ■ Italy

An attractive aroma of liquorice and ripe plums is carried through to the taste. Mature flavour with a hint of chocolate on the finish. Great with cheese and onion pie, beef stew or spicy pasta.

Shiraz-Cabernet, Bin 35, Penfolds, 1992

■ £4.39 ■ Australia

A really rich red with lots of black cherry fruitiness. An immensely powerful, flavourful wine which would go with the richest game.

SWEET WHITE

Moscatel de Valencia, Safeway

■ £3.19 ■ Spain

Sold in a frosted bottle, this is a very elegant, 15.5% alcohol, Moscatel with a subtle chocolate-orange like aroma and luscious, rich, ginger cake fruit on the palate. Exceptional value for money.

Premières Côtes de Bordeaux, Ginestet, Safeway

■ £4.29 ■ France

Golden-orange in colour, this smells just like a piece of freshly toasted bread and has a rich, honeyed, raisiny fruit flavour with a hint of orange on the finish. Drink chilled with treacle tart.

DRY SPARKLING WHITE

BB Club Brut, Balaton Boglár, Hungary

■ £4.49 ■ Hungary

Produced on the southern shores of Lake Balaton, this is an unusually flavoured sparkler that may not be to everyone's taste. It has an elderflower-like aroma and is very floral but finishes dry. Nice for a change, providing you like your fizz perfumed and fruity.

SWEET SPARKLING WHITE

Lambrusco Bianco Light, Safeway

■ £1.59 ■ Italy

Light and fizzy, this is conveniently low in alcohol at 3%. It's grapey and sweet, but nicely balanced.

SPARKLING RED

Lambrusco Rosso, Safeway

■ £2.55 ■ Italy

Earthy and jammy with a pleasant, almost peppery, violet character. There's also good fruitiness and a touch of sweetness with balancing acidity. Would go down well with Indian, Chinese or even Thai food.

Vintages and Prices
Whilst every care has been taken to ensure that vintages and prices of wines detailed in *Check it Out* are the same as those on sale, it is possible that some will have changed. If a more recent vintage is in stock, the quality should be comparable, and therefore a similar buy. (With the majority of whites, especially light and medium-dry whites, a rule of thumb is 'the younger the vintage, the fresher the wine'.)

SAINSBURY'S

★★★ STAR BUYS ★★★

Sauvignon Blanc, Cuvée Ryman, Villa Montes

■ £3.99 ■ Chile ■ Star White

Star winemaker Hugh Ryman has applied his magic wand to this wine. It has an attractive nettle-like aroma and lots of fresh, very moreish, dry, zippy, yet not aggressive fruit flavours. Drink with soup or white fish.

Merlot, Vin de Pays d'Oc, Chais Baumière, 1992

■ £3.99 ■ France ■ Star Red

An Australian makes this wine in the south of France. It combines the flavour of minty violets with lots of powerful, full-bodied fruit flavours. Attractively soft and easy to drink. Serve it with or in stew. Excellent value for money.

Wines by Style

LIGHT DRY WHITE

Baden Dry, Badischer Winzerkeller, Sainsbury's

■ £2.99 ■ Germany

The south of Germany has more sunshine than the north and therefore produces wines more French in style than German. This is a crisp, fresh, dry white wine with light, floral overtones. Delicious served with roast chicken.

Bianco di Custoza GIV, 1992

■ £3.49 ■ Italy

Produced in northern Italy from vines growing in the Veneto hills, this wine is dry, with an attractive flowery flavour and a citrus tang on the finish. Excellent with grilled fish, pasta or very lightly curried dishes.

Chardonnay-Sauvignon Blanc Reserve, Vintage Blend, Khan Krum, 1990

■ £2.99 ■ Bulgaria

This wine smells just like freshly toasted bread and has lots of deliciously rounded whitecurrant flavour. Tastes good served with sweet-and-sour fish, prawns, chicken or pork.

Colombard, Swartland, Sainsbury's

■ £3.35 ■ South Africa

Green, grassy aroma followed by crisp, dry, mouth-watering fruit flavour. On the aftertaste there is a hint of nutmeg and butter. Serve with cheese and onion pie or bacon omelette.

Corbières, Sainsbury's

■ £2.79 ■ France

Easy-drinking, dry party white, perfect to mix with soda for spritzers or with cassis (blackcurrant liqueur) to make kir.

Entre-Deux-Mers, Château La Rose du Pin, 1992

■ £4.25 ■ France

The name of this wine's region translates literally as 'between two seas'; to be more exact, the grapes are actually grown between two rivers, the River Dordogne and the River Garonne. With nice, dry, rounded fruit flavour, it could be the name that does it but this wine seems to be a better match for seafood than the other conventional partner from the Loire, Muscadet.

Est! Est!! Est!!!, Graffitti, Lugi Bigi, 1992

■ £3.99 ■ Italy

A travelling Bishop Fugger in 1111 instructed his servant to go on ahead and mark inn doors with 'est' if they sold wine. Those that sold excellent wine were marked 'est! est!! est!!!', or so goes the story. This is a crisp, appley white with lots of zippy flavour and an aftertaste of Granny Smith apples. Serve with plaice or sole.

Gentil, Hugel, 1992

■ £4.95 ■ France

Look out for Hugel's distinctive deep yellow label and you'll find it easy to spot this tall, fluted (German-looking) bottle on the supermarket shelf. Made from a mixture of the Alsace grape varieties, this is a pleasant, spicy, easy-drinking wine. Serve with lightly curried dishes or fruit-cake or serve it chilled on its own.

Hungarian Country White Wine, Southern Balaton Boglár Region, Sainsbury's

■ £2.39 ■ Hungary

From southwest of Budapest, this has attractive floral aromas and dry, almost minty fruit flavour. Serve with herb dishes like pasta and pesto or herb omelettes.

Muscadet de Sèvre-et-Maine Sur Lie, Château de la Dimerie, Sainsbury's, 1992

■ £3.99 ■ France

Rich, attractive, bready, yeast-like aromas. Zippy without being aggressive with a dry fruit flavour. Delicious with seafood or hot crispy bacon salad.

Muskat & Ugni Blanc, Country Wine, Slaviantzi, Sainsbury's

■ £2.69 ■ Bulgaria

A spicy, grapey wine which is soft and very easy to drink. Serve as an aperitif or with spicy Thai or Chinese food. At this price it is a great party wine.

Saumur Blanc, Domaine des Hauts de Sanziers, 1991

■ £4.95 ■ France

Good tangy flavours of lemons and pears. This has richer fruit than some. Serve with vegetable risotto.

Sauvignon, Vin de Pays d'Oc, Domaine St-Marc, Sainsbury's, 1992

■ £3.59 ■ France

Produced near the medieval town of Carcassonne, this

is dry and soft with tangy, easy-drinking, melon-like, slightly herbaceous fruit flavour. Drink with mussels.

Sauvignon Blanc, Chais Baumière, 1992

■ £3.99 ■ France

Made by an Australian in the Languedoc-Roussillon region of southern France, you could be forgiven for thinking this wine was from 'down under'. Masses of tropical fruit aroma jumps out of the glass, followed by ripe, luscious, soft-fruit flavour. Serve with any meat or fish in a fruit sauce.

Sauvignon Blanc, Cuvée Ryman, Villa Montes

■ £3.99 ■ Chile

Star winemaker Hugh Ryman has applied his magic wand to this wine. It has an attractive nettle-like aroma and lots of fresh, very moreish, zippy, dry (but not aggressive) fruit flavours. Drink with soup or white fish.

Sauvignon Blanc, Gyöngyös Estate, 1992

■ £3.35 ■ Hungary

Pronounced 'join-josh', this wine is made by the Australia-trained, France-based Englishman, Hugh Ryman. Very aromatic, almost gooseberry-like, with lots of crisp, dry, fruit flavour. Good with seafood and creamy fish dishes that need wine with decent acidity.

Sauvignon Blanc, Rueda Hermanos, Lurton, 1993

■ £3.99 ■ Spain

French winemaking gives attractive gooseberry aromas and flinty, fully-flavoured fruitiness to this wine – it in fact tastes rather like a New Zealand Sauvignon Blanc. An excellent complement to seafood pasta and great with pizzas.

Torrontes Dry White, Mendoza, Sainsbury's

■ £2.85 ■ Argentina

Made by Peter Bright, the talented Portugal-based Australian winemaker, this wine is made from Argentina's most prolific white grape, the Torrontes. It is very fruity, with lots of zippy, floral flavour. A great aperitif.

Trocken Rheinhessen, Sainsbury's

■ £2.99 ■ Germany

The word 'trocken' merely means dry, so if you normally wouldn't consider a German wine and tend to dismiss them all as medium-dry or sweet, give this one a try. The flowery, rounded fruit flavour is balanced by a zippy, appley aftertaste. Try serving it with fish pie.

Vin de Pays du Gers, Sainsbury's, 1992

■ £2.99 ■ France

Easy-drinking, attractive dry white with tangy fruit flavours. Great as a spritzer base.

Vin de Pays d'Oc, Sainsbury's

■ £2.85 ■ France

Earthy and quite rustic with an almost herbal aroma and pleasant, rounded, dry flavour. Drink with garlic olives or fish cooked with capers.

MEDIUM-DRY WHITE

Chenin Blanc, Moondah Brook Estate, 1992

■ £4.95 ■ Australia

Produced in the foothills of Western Australia's Darling Ranges north of Perth, this is a darling of a wine. Intense, smoky-bacon aroma and unusual zippy, yet slightly honeyed fruit flavours, followed by a lemony tang on the finish. Great with lemon chicken, fish pâté and bacon sandwiches.

Chenin Blanc, South African, Sainsbury's

■ £2.49 ■ South Africa

A lightly honeyed aroma and soft, flowery fruit flavour make this an ideal, anytime-drinking, party white.

Muscat Branco, João Pires, 1992

■ £4.49 ■ Portugal

A spicy, tangy, very moreish white made from the Muscat grape. While grapey and sweet on the aroma, it finishes with a citrus kick. Great with spicy Thai and Chinese food.

Piesporter Michelsberg, Sainsbury's

■ £2.89 ■ Germany

Oily, almost petroly aromas with an earthy, zippy, flowery flavour. Good with spicy chicken or with fish and chips.

Vouvray, Sainsbury's

■ £3.75 ■ France

Produced east of Tours in the Loire Valley, this has a flavour of honeyed melons with a refreshing citrus tang to the aftertaste. Serve with white river fish, chicken or turkey.

FULL-BODIED DRY WHITE

Chardonnay, Australian, Riverina, Sainsbury's

■ £3.99 ■ Australia

On the light side of full-bodied, with lemony, slightly smoky-bacon-like flavour. Good with bacon and eggs or roast chicken.

Chardonnay, Chais Baumière, 1991

■ £3.99 ■ France

This is produced by Australian winemakers in France, and Chais Baumière is Australian-owned – not surprisingly the result is a wine you could easily mistake as Australian. A rich, tropical fruit aroma is followed by dry, tangy, almost minty, whitecurrant flavours and then subtle oak overtones. A big wine, which is a good match for full-bodied food like prawns in ginger or for scallops with cream and vermouth.

Chardonnay, Chapel Hill, Hungary, 1992

■ £2.99 ■ Hungary

Produced on the shores of Lake Balaton, this wine has a rich, peppery aroma with slightly minty, apricot fruitiness. Excellent quality and value. Drink with salmon.

Chardonnay, Denman Estate, Hunter Valley, Sainsbury's, 1992

■ £4.99 ■ Australia

From the Hunter Valley, this wine has a creamy, toasted aroma and rounded, buttery dry fruit flavour. It copes impressively well with highly flavoured, barbecued dishes.

Chardonnay, Lindemans Bin 65, New South Wales, 1993

■ £4.95 ■ Australia

Attractive creamy aromas with zippy, floral fruit flavour... then follows a smoky, mouthwatering aftertaste which makes you reach for another glass. An excellent complement to char-grilled or barbecued dishes.

Chardonnay, Poverty Bay, Nobilo, 1992

■ £4.99 ■ New Zealand

An intense aroma of melons and butter is followed by powerful, smoky, zippy fruit flavour. Drink with skate and capers or fish and chips.

Chardonnay, Vin de Pays d'Oc, Ryman, 1992

■ £4.95 ■ France

Produced around Limoux in the south of France. On first sniff, this wine could easily be Australian, with a rich, smoky aroma and lots of smoked, rounded, lime fruit on the palate. In fact it is made by an Australian-trained Englishman, Hugh Ryman. Serve with barbecued or smoked chicken.

Chardonnay delle Tre Venezie, Sainsbury's

■ £3.59 ■ Italy

A rich, heavily toasted aroma and smoky, yet zippy fruit on the palate combine to make this wine very moreish. Drink with seafood salad, crispy bacon salad or even a bacon sandwich.

Chardonnay-Chenin Blanc, New Zealand, Sainsbury's, 1992

■ £3.95 ■ New Zealand

Lightly honeyed aroma and flavour and buttery fruitiness. Serve with any meat with a sweet, fruity sauce.

Santa Sara, Fernão Pires, (Barrel Fermented), J P Vinhos, 1992

■ £3.95 ■ Portugal

Yeasty, slightly honey-like aroma and floral fruit with a hint of vanilla on the palate. Dry but tangy, this is an unusual white, made from the Fernão Pires grape. Serve with Cajun char-grilled dishes.

Sauvignon Blanc, Montana, Marlborough, 1993

■ £4.95 ■ New Zealand

Rich, tropical yet grassy fruit on the bouquet, followed by tangy, flinty, dry fruit flavour. A well structured wine which is delicious with kippers.

Sémillon, Riverina, Sainsbury's

■ £2.99 ■ Australia

Peppery aromas, then spicy fruit and rounded, baked pear flavour. Good with smoked fish.

Viura-Chardonnay, Navarra, Sainsbury's, 1993

■ £3.95 ■ Spain

Produced in Rioja's lesser known neighbouring region, Navarra, this is a stunner. Its rich, oaky aroma is followed by ripe, buttery, vanilla fruit flavour and a tang of lime on the finish. A classy, stylish wine. Excellent value for money. Serve with fully-flavoured dishes like chicken cooked with garlic, fish soup or fish pie.

LIGHT RED

Anjou Rouge, Sainsbury's

■ £2.99 ■ France

Don't confuse it with disappointing sweet Rosé d'Anjou, this wine is completely different. It smells of fresh strawberries with a hint of black pepper. Try it chilled, it's delicious. Good with river fish like pike and perch as well as red mullet.

Castillo de Alhambra, Tinto Cencibel, La Mancha, Sainsbury's, 1992

■ £2.99 ■ Spain

Soft, fruity red with a refreshing aroma of bubblegum. Drink with salads and mushroom omelette.

Do Campo Tinto, Sainsbury's

■ £2.99 ■ Portugal

Easy-drinking, cherry-like red, made by superstar, Portugal-based Australian winemaker Peter Bright. Can be served chilled. Good with chicken and mushroom pie.

Malbec-Cabernet, Mendoza, Argentinian, Sainsbury's

■ £2.85 ■ Argentina

Attractive, soft, plummy aromas backed up by similar fruit flavours and a lingering liquorice aftertaste. Good with light pasta dishes and cold meats.

Vin de Pays de la Dordogne, Sainsbury's

■ £2.99 ■ France

Appealing cherry aromas followed by earthy fruit flavour. A good all-rounder from this popular British holiday haunt. Try it with duck pâté.

Vin Rouge de France, Sainsbury's (1.5 litre)

■ £4.89 ■ France

Don't be put off by the plastic bottle. This is a basic, yet tasty, peppery red with lots of fruit flavour – just like the drinkable wine you can buy for next to nothing in French cafés. At the equivalent of £2.45 a bottle, it's cheap too. Serve with stews, pizzas or chilled on its own.

Vintages and Prices
Whilst every care has been taken to ensure that vintages and prices of wines detailed in *Check it Out* are the same as those on sale, it is possible that some will have changed. If a more recent vintage is in stock, the quality should be comparable, and therefore a similar buy. (With the majority of whites, especially light and medium-dry whites, a rule of thumb is 'the younger the vintage, the fresher the wine'.)

MEDIUM-BODIED RED

Cabernet Sauvignon Reserve, Lovico Suhindol, 1988

■ £2.99 ■ Bulgaria

Creamy, oaky aromas are backed up by rich, vanilla fruit and perfumed blackcurrant flavour. Serve with game or lamb and rosemary.

Cabernet-Merlot, Moldova Codru

■ £2.99 ■ Moldova

Formerly part of the USSR, Moldova is now an independent republic. Unusual, attractive aromas of cloves and spices and a spicy, mature fruit flavour. This tastes as if it cost well over a fiver. A special occasion wine, serve with roast beef.

Chianti Classico, Cecchi, 1990

■ £4.35 ■ Italy

A rich, plummy wine with masses of mouthwatering flavour and a sweet-and-sour finish. Great with spaghetti bolognaise.

Claret, Sainsbury's

■ £3.15 ■ France

Easy-drinking, curranty claret with lots of tangy, earthy, fruitiness. Serve with roast beef or lamb chops.

Côtes du Frontonnais, Château Bellevue la Forêt, 1992

■ £3.95 ■ France

Produced north of Toulouse, this is a wine with great character, ripe, spicy fruit flavours, and quite a tannic, tarry aftertaste. A good foil for barbecued food or sweet-and-sour sauce.

Côtes du Rhône, Sainsbury's

■ £2.95 ■ France

Soft, rounded, easy-drinking red with earthy, jammy overtones. Drink with beef or lamb stew.

Merlot Reserve, Lovico Suhindol, 1989

■ £2.99 ■ Bulgaria

Soft, tobacco aromas; rounded, oaky, smoky flavour; then a hint of plums. Serve with stews and casseroles.

Merlot-Cabernet Reserve, Vintage Blend, Oriachovitza, Stara Zagora Region, 1989

■ £2.99 ■ Bulgaria

Unusual floral, violet aroma followed by soft fruit flavours and an attractive, bitter-sweet finish. Serve with pasta and pesto, lamb with rosemary, or herby omelettes.

Minervois, Château de Gourgazaud, Sainsbury's, 1990

■ £3.99 ■ France

This wine both looks and tastes good with its stylish classic label depicting a gold château. Deep, inky-black in colour, with masses of blackcurrants and spice on the palate. Goes especially well with oriental food, particularly Thai dishes.

Minervois, Sainsbury's

■ £2.95 ■ France

Plenty of excellent peppery smells and ripe blackberry fruit on the palate. Great with spicy Toulouse sausage, salami, or bangers and mash.

Montepulciano d'Abruzzo, Sainsbury's

■ £2.99 ■ Italy

A ripe, powerful wine, with a rich, earthy flavour. Great with game or fruit-cake.

Pinot Noir, Romania, Sainsbury's

■ £2.99 ■ Romania

An earthy red with ripe strawberry aromas and flavours and an attractive tang of acidity. Could be drunk chilled. Try it with lamb or pork.

Sicilian Red, Sainsbury's

■ £2.69 ■ Italy

A stylish red with soft, cherry fruitiness and attractive, mouth-filling flavours. Serve with roast beef or lamb.

Spanna del Piemonte, Sainsbury's

■ £2.99 ■ Italy

Creamy, vanilla aromas, cherry-like flavour and bitter tannin. Good with sweet-and-sour pork or chicken.

Tempranillo-Cabernet Sauvignon, Navarra, Sainsbury's, 1990

■ £3.95 ■ Spain

This wine is a stunner! Aged in small oak casks it has a rich, vanilla, ripe blackcurrants aroma and flavour. Very moreish. Serve with roast beef and game.

Valdepeñas Reserva, Bodegas Felix Solis, Sainsbury's, 1988

■ £3.29 ■ Spain

Don't worry if you've never heard of this Spanish red, wait until you taste it! Its ripe flavour of black cherries makes it hard to resist and, while massively fruity, it has both a touch of sweetness and a good kick of acidity on the finish. Try it with roast or Peking-style duck.

Vinho de Mesa, Arruda, Sainsbury's

■ £2.79 ■ Portugal

A best-selling rough-and-ready, earthy red from north-east of Lisbon. Ideal with spicy and barbecued food.

FULL-BODIED RED

Alentejo, Herdade de Santa Marta, J P Vinhos, 1991

■ £3.99 ■ Portugal

Complex fruit flavours and violet aromas make this an easy-drinking velvety red. Tastes good with smoked fish dishes like kedgeree, as well as garlicky meats.

Cabernet Sauvignon, Nottage Hill, Hardy's, 1992

■ £3.99 ■ Australia

Beefy, minty red with lots of mouth-filling fruit flavour.

A perfect foil for anything meaty like beef and onion pie, hefty beefburgers with relish or a hot, fiery chilli.

Cabernet Sauvignon, Vin de Pays d'Oc, Chais Baumière, 1991

■ £3.99 ■ France

Produced in the Languedoc-Roussillon region of France, this tastes a bit like an Australian red – possibly something do with the fact that the wine is owned and made by Australians. It has good structure and lots of floral blackcurrant flavour. Delicious with really ripe soft cheese.

Cabernet-Shiraz, Rosemount Estate, 1991

■ £4.95 ■ Australia

Look for the diamond shaped label on this stunning Aussie red. Spicy, berry-like fruit, a touch of sweetness, and lots of blackcurrant and vanilla flavours make it remarkable value and quality for money.

Copertino Riserva, Cantina Sociale Coop Copertino, Sainsbury's, 1990

■ £3.95 ■ Italy

There's lots of oaky, plummy flavour and a hint of spice in this mature, stylish Italian red. Ideal with rich stews and casseroles.

Corbières, Domaine du Réverend, 1989

■ £3.99 ■ France

Very earthy, rustic red with lots of ripe, blackcurrant flavour and plenty of hard tannin. Tastes softer when decanted. Serve with game or cheese and onion pie.

Faugères, Sainsbury's

■ £2.99 ■ France

Plenty of delicious robust southern French fruitiness characterizes this straightforward, easy-drinking, plummy red. Full-bodied without being too tannic. Try a bottle with *coq au vin.*

Graves Sélection, Louis Vialard, Sainsbury's

■ £3.95 ■ France

Produced from Merlot and Cabernet Sauvignon, to the south of Bordeaux, this is a classic red with ripe, liquoricy, spicy overtones. A touch of oak on the finish makes it a very stylish claret. Serve with roast lamb or beef and strong cheese.

Merlot, Vin de Pays d'Oc, Chais Baumière, 1992

■ £3.99 ■ France

An Australian makes this wine in the south of France. It combines minty violet flavours with lots of powerful, full-bodied fruit character. Attractively soft and easy to drink. Serve it with or in stew. Excellent value for money.

Shiraz, Bin 822, Wyndham Estate, Sainsbury's, 1992

■ £4.59 ■ Australia

Straightforward, easy-drinking smooth red with lots of juicy fruit flavour but not too much bitter tannin. Good with tomato-based pasta dishes.

Shiraz-Cabernet, Hardy's Stamp Series, 1993

■ £3.59 ■ Australia

This wine is consistently good. It's easy to spot on the shelf – look for the label with the kangaroo stamp on it. It has lots of earthy, vanilla flavour and a slightly smoky aftertaste. Great with barbecued or smoked food.

SWEET WHITE

Bernkasteler Kürfurstlay Spätlese, Sainsbury's, 1992

■ £3.99 ■ Germany

Produced in the Mosel Valley from ripe Riesling grapes, this wine has a honeysuckle aroma and rich, oily, sweet fruitiness, leaving an attractive dry tang in the mouth. A classy aperitif to be drunk lightly chilled.

Moscatel de Valencia, Sainsbury's

■ £2.89 ■ Spain

Sold in a frosted bottle. Like luscious (15% alcohol) liquid marmalade, with blockbusting raisiny flavour. Pour it over vanilla or rum and raisin ice-cream.

Vintages and Prices

Whilst every care has been taken to ensure that vintages and prices of wines detailed in *Check it Out* are the same as those on sale, it is possible that some will have changed. If a more recent vintage is in stock, the quality should be comparable, and therefore a similar buy. (With the majority of whites, especially light and medium-dry whites, a rule of thumb is 'the younger the vintage, the fresher the wine'.)

DRY SPARKLING WHITE

Sparkling Wine, Seppelt, Sainsbury's

■ £4.99 ■ Australia

There is a slightly tropical fruit aroma and flavour to this stylish dry, rounded fizz. Made by Seppelt, whose Great Western Brut Reserve is stocked by Gateway, KwikSave, Morrisons and Waitrose.

DRY ROSE

Bordeaux Clairet, Sainsbury's

■ £2.99 ■ France

No, this wine's name is not a misprint, it is the traditional spelling for claret, which used to be dark rosé in colour like this wine. It's made from the classic claret grapes (Cabernet Sauvignon and Merlot) and has all the same ripe, blackcurrant-like, tangy fruitiness of the famous red, without the bitter tannin. Great with flavourful vegetarian dishes, and almost anything else.

Cabernet Sauvignon Rosé, Nagyrede, Sainsbury's

■ £2.99 ■ Hungary

From northeast of Budapest. Slightly sweet, but leaving a refreshingly dry, red fruit flavour.

Côtes du Lubéron Rosé, Domaine des Blancs, Sainsbury's, 1992

■ £4.59 ■ France

Subtly dry and tangy, this pinky orange coloured rosé

is produced from grapes grown in the Vaucluse area. Will stand up to strong flavours like olives.

Merlot Rosé, Vin de Pays d'Oc, Domaine de la Tuilerie, 1992

■ £3.99 ■ France

A spicy rosé with a rounded fruit flavour and an unusual spicy finish. A good foil for really herby dishes. Made by superstar 'flying winemaker' Hugh Ryman.

SPARKLING RED

Nivola, Lambrusco Mantovano Secco

■ £2.99 ■ Italy

Attractive, earthy, tangy fizz with moreish zippy red fruit flavours and a refreshing dry finish. Ideal with pastas, pâté and soups, or as an unusual aperitif.

TESCO

★★★ STAR BUYS ★★★

Semillon-Sauvignon, McLaren Vale, International Winemaker, Tesco, 1992

■ £4.99 ■ Australia ■ Star White

Made by talented French winemaker, Jacques Lurton, this is a stunning oak-aged white with an attractive vanilla-like aroma. Lots of rich, dry fruit flavour with a hint of cinnamon makes it ideal with spicy food, or meat with fruit-based sauces.

Cabernet Sauvignon Reserve, Suhindol, Tesco, 1988

■ £3.49 ■ Bulgaria ■ Star Red

An intensely rich aroma of blackcurrants and lots of big, gutsy fruit flavour combine to make this wine an amazing bargain. Will make even the simplest supper seem impressive. Drink with roast beef or pizza.

Wines by Style

LIGHT DRY WHITE

Australian White, Tesco

■ £2.99 ■ Australia

Recognize this wine by the crocodile on the label. Nice, soft, rounded fruitiness with a lemony bite. Serve with smoked fish like haddock or kedgeree.

Chardonnay Reserve, Khan Krum, Bulgarian, Tesco, 1990

■ £3.49 ■ Bulgaria

Delicious buttery flavours with soft vanilla overtones. Tastes like a £5 bottle of wine. Great served with chicken tikka.

Chardonnay, Robertson, Tesco, 1993

■ £3.99 ■ South Africa

Produced in Robertson, east of the Cape Peninsula, this has soft, rounded fruit flavour with an attractive mouthwatering citrus tang on the finish. Drink with creamy fish dishes and pasta.

Chardonnay, Vin de Pays d'Oc, Domaine du Bois, 1992

■ £3.79 ■ France

Rich and lightly honeyed, this is rather like an Aussie Chardonnay with intense, exotic fruit flavours. Easy-drinking and good value for money. Great with char-grilled or barbecued food.

Chardonnay-Sémillon, Maipo, Chilean, Tesco

■ £3.99 ■ Chile

This wine not only has a zany label, but an unusual flavour too. Creamy fruit combines with dry, zippy, citrus-like notes. Try it with creamy fish dishes.

Colli Toscana, Tesco

■ £3.29 ■ Italy

An oddity and very much an acquired taste. It has a

strong, almost meaty aroma with dry, lightly earthy, rounded fruit flavours. Great with chicken and leek pie.

Nuragus di Cagliari, Tesco

■ £3.29 ■ Italy

Produced in southern Sardinia, this has an unusual perfumed, floral aroma with crisp, pear-like flavour on the palate. The flavour is heightened by a slight spritz. An excellent aperitif.

Pinot Bianco, Cormons, 1992

■ £4.29 ■ Italy

Unusual and exciting wine with tropical perfumed aromas and lots of floral, zippy fruit flavour. Serve with any herby dish, like lamb and rosemary, pasta or spicy pizza.

Rueda, International Winemaker, Tesco, 1992

■ £3.69 ■ Spain

Made by a Frenchman (Jacques Lurton) in Spain, this has lots of zippy, dry, rounded fruit character with a hint of honeyed richness on the finish. A good all-rounder.

Saumur Blanc, Caves des Vignerons de Saumur, Tesco

■ £2.99 ■ France

You don't find much still white from this part of the Loire in Britain, but its worth looking out for this one. Lots of floral, honeysuckle-like flavour with a dry, yet flowery aftertaste. Try it with cheese soufflé or omelette.

Semillon-Sauvignon, McLaren Vale, International Winemaker, Tesco, 1992

■ £4.99 ■ Australia

Made by talented French winemaker, Jacques Lurton, this is a stunning oak-aged white with an attractive vanilla-like aroma. Lots of rich, dry, fruit flavour with a hint of cinnamon makes it ideal with spicy food, or meat with fruit-based sauces.

South African Dry White, International Winemaker, Tesco

■ £2.99 ■ South Africa

Lots of tangy, gooseberry fruit character with a slightly honeyed aftertaste. Verging towards medium-dry. Drink with fish and chips.

Vin de Pays de l'Aude, Dorgan White Wine

■ £2.79 ■ France

Zippy, refreshing dry fruitiness. At this price it's a very affordable everyday or party wine.

Vin de Pays des Côtes de Gascogne, Escoubes, Grassa, Tesco

■ £2.99 ■ France

This wine is consistently good, year in, year out. Crisp, sherbet-like flavours are backed up by a tangy, fruity aftertaste. Goes surprisingly well with pork.

Vin de Pays des Côtes du Tarn, Domaine St-Alain, Tesco, 1993

■ £3.29 ■ France

This domaine has been producing wine since the 16th century, but don't worry, this wine doesn't taste that old! Good party white with gulpable dry fruit flavour.

MEDIUM-DRY WHITE

Chenin Blanc, Cape, Stellenbosch, Tesco

■ £3.29 ■ South Africa

Tangy, appley, moreish flavour. Fairly dry for a medium-dry style. Serve with chicken or fish and chips.

Chenin Blanc, Western Australia, Tesco, 1992

■ £4.99 ■ Australia

Attractive, sherbet-like wine with unusual peachy flavours and a touch of citrus on the finish. Great with soups, crispy bacon salad or turkey.

Orvieto Abboccato, Tesco

■ £3.49 ■ Italy

Rounded, attractive, sweetish fruit flavours with a refreshing zip of acidity. Drink with fruit and pastries.

Rhine Riesling, Australia, Tesco

■ £3.49 ■ Australia

An easy-drinking white with floral aromas and zippy, perfumed flavour. A great aperitif or picnic wine.

Riesling Mosel, Tesco

■ £2.99 ■ Germany

Look for the clear, high-shouldered, Bordeaux-shaped bottle and the blue and turquoise label.

Luscious honey aromas, with tangy, dry, steely fruit on the palate. Very moreish, a great aperitif.

Steinweiler Kloster Liebfrauenberg Kabinett, Pfalz, Tesco

■ £3.99 ■ Germany

Look for the clear, high-shouldered, Bordeaux-shaped bottle. A honeyed wine with zippy, lemony flavour. Great with blue cheese or skate wings with capers.

Vouvray, Tesco

■ £3.99 ■ France

Honey-like, appley fruit characterizes this wine from the Loire Valley. Ideal as an aperitif, or drunk with fish pâté, chicken or fruit salad. A very versatile wine.

FULL-BODIED DRY WHITE

Chardonnay, Gisborne, Tesco

■ £4.79 ■ New Zealand

A zippy, herbaceous white with crisp fruit flavour and good acidity. Very different to (often clumsier) Australian Chardonnay, with an earthy, smoky taste. Serve with smoked fish or meat, mackerel pâté or spicy soup.

Gewurztraminer, Alsace, Tesco, 1992

■ £4.99 ■ France

Produced in northern France, this is a wine for those who like exotic flavours. Rich, floral lychees on the nose are followed by tropical flavours which at first you expect to be sweet but finish dry and tangy. Great with spicy dishes, sweet-and-sour pork or smoked fish.

Marqués de Chivé White, Tesco

■ £2.99 ■ Spain

From the east coast of Spain, this is a big wine with lots of vanilla overtones and a rich, buttery taste. Not subtle, but a good complement to fish pie, or anything flavoured with saffron, which can obliterate many a wine.

Rioja, Viña Mara, Tesco

■ £3.95 ■ Spain

Rich vanilla aroma with masses of upfront fruitiness and quite dry flavour. Well balanced wine which tastes as if it cost twice its price. Try it with squid or prawns.

Viognier, Vin de Pays d'Oc, Domaine St-James, 1992

■ £4.99 ■ France

This is an unusual grape variety you'll either love or hate. An intense aroma of pineapples and bananas is followed by tangy, tropical fruit flavours with a hint of coconut. The ideal foil to spicy Thai food rich in coconut, lime leaves, lemon grass and chillis.

LIGHT RED

Blauerzwiegelt, 1992

■ £3.69 ■ Austria

Light, tangy red which smells and tastes of redcurrants. Serve chilled. Great for parties, barbecues and picnics.

Cabernet Sauvignon-Merlot, Riverlea, Gisborne, Tesco, 1990

■ £3.99 ■ New Zealand

Unusual earthy, stalky aroma with smoky, tangy fruit flavour. Good with smoked chicken or smoked bacon.

Dornfelder, Rheinpfalz, Tesco

■ £2.99 ■ Germany

A good wine to start with if you've yet to try German red. An unusual, lightly spicy wine, with rounded, lightly peppery fruitiness. Could be served chilled. A good party wine, and great value for money at the equivalent price of £2.24 for a normal 75cl bottle.

Malbec-Cabernet, Mendoza, Uvas del Sol

■ £3.99 ■ Argentina

This wine has a strong blackcurrant aroma and quite creamy, yet zippy, dry fruit flavour. Serve chilled as an aperitif or picnic wine or with steak sandwiches.

Villa Pigna Superiore, Rosso Piceno, 1989

■ £3.49 ■ Italy

Tangy flavours, like red fruit gums, then lots of earthy, spicy acidity on the finish. Great with cold meats.

MEDIUM-BODIED RED

Buzet, Domaine de la Croix, Tesco, 1989

■ £3.99 ■ France

Years ago this region was part of Bordeaux and it still uses the same blend of grapes. Masses of firm cassis fruit flavour combines with a ripe, creamy yet tannic finish. Excellent with duck.

Cabernet Sauvignon, Auckland, Tesco

■ £4.79 ■ New Zealand

A tangy, earthy red with slightly spicy blackcurrant flavours. Ideal with smoked chicken.

Cabernet Sauvignon, Maipo, Tesco

■ £3.99 ■ Chile

This wine has a distinct aroma of eucalyptus followed by beefy blackcurrant fruit flavour. Towards the heavier side of medium-bodied, serve with strong cheese or venison.

Cabernet Sauvignon, Suhindol Region, Bulgaria, Tesco

■ £2.85 ■ Bulgaria

Easy-drinking red with cherry-stone flavour and soft, velvety fruitiness with a hint of tobacco. Like an old-fashioned claret. Serve with rich stews and casseroles.

Cabernet Sauvignon-Merlot, International Winemaker, Tesco

■ £3.99 ■ South Africa

A spicy, earthy red with a fresh, vigorous flavour of blackcurrants. Serve with spicy meat dishes.

Chianti Classico, Tesco, 1991

■ £3.99 ■ Italy

Look for the two-tone red and marbled slate coloured

label. A rich chocolate aroma and ripe, chocolate and raisin flavours. Very moreish. Serve with roast beef, venison or strong blue cheese.

Côtes du Lubéron, Domaine des Baumelles, Tesco, 1992

■ £4.29 ■ France

This wine is extremely aromatic, rather like pink sherbet! Lots of medium-bodied fruit flavour, backed by a hint of Mediterranean spice. Excellent with pasta and pesto, spaghetti bolognaise or pasta with a garlic and tomato sauce.

Merlot, Maipo, Santa Rita, Chilean, Tesco

■ £3.99 ■ Chile

It is hard to resist this wine after just one whiff of its ripe plums and violets and one taste of its velvety, plummy fruit. Serve with pasta to make even the most ordinary meal taste exciting.

Merlot del Piave, Tesco

■ £2.99 ■ Italy

Produced in the Veneto region of northeast Italy, this wine has masses of soft, easy-drinking, plummy fruit flavour. Very moreish. Serve with pot roasts or casseroles.

Pinot Noir, Baden, 1990

■ £4.49 ■ Germany

If you've never tried a German red, this is the wine to start with. Spot it by looking for the French-style burgundy-shaped bottle. It's like ripe strawberries with a hint of cream. An excellent complement to roast lamb or pork.

Pinot Noir del Veneto, Tesco

■ £2.99 ■ Italy

A fun wine that smells and tastes like Bazooka bubblegum and summer pudding with a curranty, citrus tang. Serve chilled with chilli chicken, picnics or barbecues.

Shiraz-Cabernet Sauvignon, Australian Red, Southeast Australia, Tesco

■ £2.99 ■ Australia

Look for the kangaroo on the label. A rich wine with lots of rounded, spicy flavour. Try it with spicy, garlicky chicken, pizza or grilled sardines.

Uvas del Sol, Argentinian Red

■ £3.49 ■ Argentina

This has both an unusual, arty label and an unusually good flavour! Plums combine with a chocolate fruit character to make it extremely moreish. Try it with Stilton, mature Cheddar or chocolate mousse.

FULL-BODIED RED

Cabernet Sauvignon Reserve, Suhindol, Tesco, 1988

■ £3.49 ■ Bulgaria

An intensely rich aroma of blackcurrants and lots of big, gutsy fruit flavour combine to make this wine an amazing bargain. Will make even the simplest supper seem impressive. Drink with roast beef or pizza.

Cabernet Sauvignon, Nottage Hill, Hardy's, 1991

■ £4.39 ■ Australia

Beefy, minty red with lots of mouth-filling fruit. The perfect foil for anything really meaty like beef and onion pie, hefty beefburgers with relish or a hot, fiery chilli dish.

Claret, Vintage, Bordeaux Supérieur, Yvon Mau, Tesco, 1990

■ £4.79 ■ France

Rich, liquorice aromas with quite austere, enticing fruit flavour. The tannin would be softened by decanting this wine. Perfect with roast beef.

Côtes du Rhône-Villages, Domaine de Prebayon, 1992

■ £4.49 ■ France

One of the stars of this book, with a very intense, chocolatey aroma and delicious, ripe, full, spicy fruit flavour. Tastes like a £10 bottle. It's ideal with rich casseroles, yet it also has the guts to stand up to ethnic spicy food.

Don Darias

■ £2.69 ■ Spain

Lots of spicy, peppery fruit with an unusual but attractive nutty, cherry-like flavour. Excellent value for money. Very easy to drink on its own, this is a deservedly popular wine that goes well with most food too.

Syrah, Vin de Pays d'Oc, International Winemaker, Tesco, 1992

■ £4.99 ■ France

Made by Jacques Lurton, a well known Bordeaux producer, this is southern French red at its best with lots of mouthwatering, spicy fruit flavours. A refreshing touch of acidity on the finish completes it. Very moreish.

Toro, Tesco, 1990

■ £3.99 ■ Spain

Produced in northern Spain, Toro is a name worth remembering. A big and plummy wine with masses of fruit flavour, full-bodied and easy-drinking. Copes well with Thai or Indian food.

Zinfandel, Californian, Tesco

■ £3.99 ■ USA

This has all the vanilla smells of a Rioja, but with far greater intensity. It has an unusual roasted creamy berry-like flavour and bitter aftertaste. Serve with venison, pheasant, pigeon or grouse.

SWEET WHITE

Premières Côtes de Bordeaux, Tesco

■ £3.99 ■ France

Produced from Sémillon and Sauvignon Blanc grapes, southeast of the city of Bordeaux, this has an attractive fruit-cake aroma and rounded sweet flavour with a tang of acidity on the finish. Delicious with bread-and-butter pudding.

Steinweiler Kloster Liebfrauenberg Auslese, Tesco

■ £4.99 ■ Germany

Produced from naturally sweet grapes grown in the Pfalz, this is a spicy wine with rich fruit flavours, rather like a liquid fruit-cake. Try serving it chilled with a slice of the latter!

Vin de Pays des Côtes de Gascogne, Domaine de la Jalousie Late Harvest, Yves Grassa, 1990

■ £4.49 ■ France

This is a Vin de Pays des Côtes de Gascogne with a difference in that the grapes were picked very ripe, late on in the harvest, and as a result the wine is sweet rather than dry. Its rich, enticing floral aroma and sherbet-like, sweet fruit taste are balanced by a refreshing tang on the finish.

DRY SPARKLING WHITE

Australian Sparkling Brut, Tesco

■ £4.99 ■ Australia

Lively fizz with an attractive yeasty aroma and quite a creamy, appley flavour. Could be drunk equally well on its own or with any light- to medium-flavoured dish.

DRY ROSE

Cabernet de Saumur, Tesco

■ £3.49 ■ France

A Loire Valley wine from the distinctive, strawberry-like, earthy Cabernet Franc grape. Serve chilled, and try it with lamb. The bottle has a seal on its neck.

SWEET ROSE

Red Muscadelle, Blanc de Noirs, Van Loveren, 1993

■ £3.29 ■ South Africa

Certainly the most unusual rosé in this book, it has an extraordinary perfumed aroma (reminded me of Brillcream!) with rounded, sweet, yet tangy fruit flavour. Ideal drunk with, or poured over, puddings.

Vintages and Prices

Whilst every care has been taken to ensure that vintages and prices of wines detailed in *Check it Out* are the same as those on sale, it is possible that some will have changed. If a more recent vintage is in stock, the quality should be comparable, and therefore a similar buy. (With the majority of whites, especially light and medium-dry whites, a rule of thumb is 'the younger the vintage, the fresher the wine'.)

WAITROSE

★★★ STAR BUYS ★★★

Sauvignon Blanc, Oxford Landing, Yalumba, 1993

■ £4.79 ■ Australia ■ Star White

This stylishly labelled and flavoured wine has a zippy, lime cordial-like flavour with lots of attractive dry fruitiness. Named after a site where drovers grazed and watered sheep on their way to Adelaide from the north. Good with sprats, sardines and prawns.

Rioja, Cosme Palacio y Hermanos, 1990

■ £4.55 ■ Spain ■ Star Red

It's apt that this wine is named after one of Rioja's pioneers. Rich, with vanilla overtones, it has masses of ripe fruit flavour and a creamy finish. Drink with well-seasoned chicken, or lamb chops.

Wines by Style

LIGHT DRY WHITE

Baden Dry, Badischer Winzerkeller

■ £3.25 ■ Germany

Produced in the sunny south of Germany, this is a wine with a lightly honeyed aroma and crisp, flowery fruit flavours. It's a delicious complement to savoury pancakes.

Blanc de Mer, Vin de Table, Pierre Guery

■ £2.85 ■ France

As the name of this wine suggests, it goes very well with seafood. Crisp, refreshing, dry, with attractive, slightly minty flavours. Excellent value for money.

Bordeaux, Château du Rival, (Oak Aged), Michel Lafon, 1992

■ £3.75 ■ France

Soft vanilla aromas and dry, almost minty, fruitiness. A stylish and balanced white, ideal with slightly spicy dishes like satay with peanut sauce.

Bordeaux Blanc, Château Chaubinet, Ryman, 1992

■ £3.95 ■ France

Delicious soft, rounded wine made from 100% Sémillon grapes and which smells of bananas! Enticing and easy-drinking – makes a perfect aperitif.

Bordeaux Sec, Château Haut-Rian, 1992

■ £3.99 ■ France

Dry and zippy, with crisp gooseberry flavour. Refreshingly tart, so ideal with seafood, especially mussels and prawns.

Bourgogne Aligoté, Domaine St-Clair, Brocard, 1992

■ £4.99 ■ France

Aligoté can be a very harsh, acidic grape variety. Happily, this example is not! Ripe and refreshing, with quite rich fruit flavour, it can be enjoyed on its own or mixed with cassis (blackcurrant liqueur) to make a kir.

Gaillac Blanc, Cave de Labastide de Levis, 1992

■ £3.49 ■ France

If you are bored with the sameness of dry whites, give Gaillac a go. An unusual pineapple aroma is followed by dry yet tropical flavours with a touch of peaches. Serve it with any meat dish with a fruit sauce or with fruit salad.

Muscadet de Sèvre-et-Maine, Pierre Guery, Waitrose, 1992

■ £2.99 ■ France

Crisp, tangy tastes which cannot offend, with a dry, lightly perfumed finish. Good with chicken broth.

Nuragus di Cagliari, Waitrose, 1992

■ £3.29 ■ Italy

A Sardian white whose grape, the Nuragus, is named after the island's prehistoric stone towers. Crisp, appley flavour with a light, refreshing zip of acidity on the finish. Excellent with vegetable risotto and seafood pasta.

Sauvignon Blanc, Oxford Landing, Yalumba, 1993

■ £4.79 ■ Australia

This stylishly labelled wine has a zippy, lime cordial-like flavour with lots of attractive dry fruitiness.

Named after a site where drovers grazed and watered sheep on their way to Adelaide from the north. Good with sprats, sardines and prawns.

Touraine Sauvignon, Domaine Gibault, 1992

■ £3.99 ■ France

Look for the fleur-de-lys seal on this bottle. Crisp and gooseberry-like, this is a wine with dry zippiness complemented by mouthwatering, moreish fruit. Drink with white fish like plaice or sole.

Vintage White, Bel Arbors, 1992

■ £3.49 ■ USA

Attractive floral aroma, easy-drinking dryness, then tangy citrus notes. Drink with creamy chicken dishes.

MEDIUM-DRY WHITE

Bereich Bernkastel, Waitrose', 1992

■ £2.79 ■ Germany

Appealingly perfumed aroma and zippy fruit flavours with a lemony tang on the finish. Great party wine.

Bereich Bernkastel Kabinett, Waitrose, 1992

■ £3.39 ■ Germany

Rich, luscious aromas and earthy, lemony, tangy, honeyed flavours. Try it with lemon meringue pie.

Bereich Bingen Kabinett, Rheinhessen, Waitrose, 1992

■ £3.39 ■ Germany

Attractive flavours like Granny Smith apples cooked in sugar. Try with smoked salmon or smoked chicken.

Dexheimer Doktor Spätlese, 1992

■ £3.75 ■ Germany

This has a wonderful honeyed aroma and luscious, honey-like yet tangy fruit on the palate. Excellent value for money. Great with fruit tart or fish pâté.

Hochheimer Holle Riesling Kabinett, Wernesches, Rheingau, 1990

■ £4.99 ■ Germany

Rich, raisiny wine with honeyed overtones and a refreshing zip of acidity on the finish. Delicious with roast or lemon chicken.

Liebfraumilch, Waitrose

■ £2.49 ■ Germany

Distinctive, creamy aroma and rich, honeyed flavour. Great elegance. Serve with scallops, prawns or paella.

Ockfener Bockstein Riesling, Wagner, 1992

■ £4.99 ■ Germany

Zippy, sherbety wine with earthy, tangy overtones. Very stylish. Good with veal or seafood pasta.

Piesporter Michelsberg, Waitrose, 1992

■ £2.99 ■ Germany

This stylish wine has a slight spritz with a honeyed, flowery flavour and an aftertaste of zippy apples. Serve with fish pâté, chicken soup or roast turkey.

Riesling, Mosel, Waitrose, 1992

■ £2.99 ■ Germany

Spritzy wine with apricot fruit flavours and a crisp, dry, lemony tang. Nice aperitif.

FULL-BODIED DRY WHITE

Chardonnay, Cartlidge and Browne

■ £4.99 ■ USA

Rich, creamy aroma followed by buttery fruit flavour and a good tang of acidity on the finish. Well balanced, easy-drinking. Serve with char-grilled meats.

Chardonnay, Koonunga Hill, Penfolds, Southeast Australia, 1993

■ £4.95 ■ Australia

A strong vanilla aroma is backed up by rich, buttery fruitiness and a zippy, lemony bite to the taste. Serve with cassoulet, roast or stir-fry chicken, or chicken soup.

Chardonnay, Le Chardon, Avontuur, Stellenbosch, 1992

■ £4.99 ■ South Africa

Light, nutty aroma, rich, creamy flavour, and a citrusy finish. Delicious with baked ham or mushroom risotto.

Chardonnay, Nottage Hill, Hardy's, Southeast Australia, 1993

■ £3.99 ■ Australia

Rich, toasted oaky flavour with buttery, citrus fruit. Good with duck or roast goose.

Chardonnay, Vin de Pays d'Oc, Philippe de Baudin, 1992

■ £4.49 ■ France

Owned by the Australian wine company Hardy's, this Chardonnay has a rich, tropical aroma with tangy, full-bodied flavour. An excellent aperitif.

Don Hugo Blanco, Bodegas Vitorianas

■ £2.79 ■ Spain

Full-bodied, easy-drinking white with dry, tangy fruit and a hint of vanilla. Even better when you consider its very reasonable price. Good with chicken pie or could cope with quite full favoured dishes like chicken satay with peanut sauce.

Rioja Blanco, Cosme Palacio y Hermanos, 1992

■ £4.55 ■ Spain

This is an acquired taste, with a rich, almost vermouth-like aroma and creamy, nutty fruit flavour. Excellent with garlicky fish soup and all the trimmings or smoked mackerel pâté.

LIGHT RED

Beaujolais-Villages, Cellier des Samsons, 1992

■ £3.99 ■ France

There's lots of juicy yet complex fruit flavour in this deliciously refreshing wine. Drink lightly chilled with soft French cheese.

Merlot-Pinot Noir, Bulgarian Country Wine, Sliven

■ £2.75 ■ Bulgaria

Attractive chocolate and plum aromas with lightly spiced, plummy fruit flavour. An easy-drinking, any-time wine and great value. Makes cheese on toast appear far more exciting.

MEDIUM-BODIED RED

Bordeaux Supérieur, Château Le Gardera, Cordier, 1990

■ £4.99 ■ France

Appealingly round, velvety fruit combines with ripe blackcurrants and plums on the finish. Impressive for its price. Delicious with beef in red wine, jugged hare, or strong French cheeses.

Buzet, Prieuré de Fonclaire, 1992

■ £3.75 ■ France

How could you fail to like a wine with this wonderful name (sounds like 'boozy'!). Lots of ripe fruit flavour with a firm, liquorice finish. Serve with steak or steak and kidney pie.

Cabernet Sauvignon, Vin de Pays de l'Aude, Foncalieu, 1992

■ £2.99 ■ France

Ripe, blackcurrant wine with masses of mouthwatering flavour. Excellent with venison, pheasant, partridge or any meat served with a fruit-based, slightly sweet sauce.

Cabernet Sauvignon, Vin de Pays d'Oc, Hugh Ryman, 1992

■ £3.99 ■ France

Superstar winemaker Hugh Ryman certainly gets around, and he always comes up with the goods too: produced near Carcassonne, this is Cabernet Sauvignon with blackcurrant fruit aroma jumping out of the glass followed by creamy vanilla and blackcurrant flavours to the taste. Try serving it with full flavoured spicy meat dishes.

Corbières, Cuvée Adélaïde, (Oak Aged), 1991

■ £3.85 ■ France

A wonderful spicy vanilla aroma with lots of rich, spicy, plummy flavour on the palate. Still quite bitter on the finish. Would soften out with decanting. Drink with full-bodied food like rabbit stew, venison, pheasant or any dish laced with garlic.

Côtes du Rhône, Château St-Maurice, 1991

■ £3.99 ■ France

This wine comes from a château whose vineyards date back to the 14th century. They obviously knew how to make wine then and still do! This is rich and spicy with masses of rounded fruit flavour. Serve with spicy Thai or Indian dishes.

Côtes du Ventoux, Les Oliviers, Boutinot, 1992

■ £2.99 ■ France

A Rhône appellation often offering better value and quality for money than the better known Côtes du

Rhône. An easy-drinking, rounded wine with spicy fruit and plummy overtones. Serve with meat pie or roast pork.

Malbec, Santa Julia, Mendoza, 1992

■ £3.75 ■ Argentina

Produced in the foothills of the Andes, this red has an attractive peppery aroma and lots of spicy, liquorice fruit flavour. Try it with steak and kidney pie or peppered steak.

Merlot, Vin de Pays d'Oc, Domaine des Fontaines, 1992

■ £2.99 ■ France

Merlot produced on the site of a fountain which used to be a staging post for thirsty travellers on their way to the mountains. It's apt that this wine is very gulpable, with masses of plummy Mediterranean fruit flavour and a ripe, sweet touch on the finish. Drink with turkey, chicken or veal.

Monica di Sardegna, Waitrose, 1992

■ £3.29 ■ Italy

An attractive wine with a floral, perfumed aroma and lots of tobacco-like, plummy fruit flavour. Ideal served with roast beef.

Rosso Conero, Umani Ronchi, 1991

■ £3.99 ■ Italy

Ripe, spicy red, with oaky overtones. Ideal with spicy sausages or liver and bacon.

Ruby Cabernet, California, 1992

■ £3.49 ■ USA

Being bottled in France doesn't seem to have affected the flavour of this jammy, blackcurranty California wine. Serve with roast beef or lamb casserole.

Syrah, Vin de Pays des Comtes Rhodaniens, 1992

■ £3.15 ■ France

Produced in the Ardèche, this wine smells and tastes like black bean sauce! Needless to say, it is something of an acquired taste, but will certainly complement Chinese dishes.

Teroldego Rotaliano, Gaierhof, 1992

■ £4.25 ■ Italy

Rich, spicy, with flavours of roasted ripe fruits. Serve with strong, mature hard cheese or roast pheasant.

Valencia, Castillo de Liria, Vincente Gandía

■ £2.65 ■ Spain

A soft, rounded cherry red from a region of Spain more famous for its oranges. Easy-drinking, curranty flavours make it ideal for parties.

Vino de Mesa, Don Hugo Tinto, Bodegas Vitorianas

■ £2.79 ■ Spain

Produced in northern Spain, this is a wine you can rely on. Lots of peppery, earthy, black fruit flavour. A good all-rounder, serve with any supper.

FULL-BODIED RED

Mavrud, Asenovgrad, 1988

■ £3.25 ■ Bulgaria

Made from local Mavrud grapes which give a rustic, fruity flavour, this is more typical of the region than Cabernet Sauvignon wines. Good with herby dishes.

Rioja, Cosme Palacio y Hermanos, 1990

■ £4.55 ■ Spain

It's apt that this wine is named after one of Rioja's pioneers. Rich, with vanilla overtones, it has masses of ripe fruit flavour and a creamy finish. Drink with well-seasoned chicken, or lamb chops.

Tinto da Anfora, João Pires, 1989

■ £4.95 ■ Portugal

A classy wine, (tastes like one worth twice the price). Soft, concentrated ripe fruit flavour (blackcurrant and raspberries) and a hint of ripe cherries on the finish.

SWEET WHITE

Moscatel de Valencia, Castillo de Liria

■ £3.15 ■ Spain

Enticing barley sugar aromas and rich, marmalade-like fruit on the palate make this a very moreish (and strong at 15% alcohol) sweet white produced in southeast Spain. The screw-top bottle makes it easy to keep in the fridge where, once opened, it will last for at least two weeks (if you can resist it) without deteriorating. Delicious with creamy, fruity puddings.

Premières Côtes de Bordeaux, Château Tour Balot, 1990

■ £4.99 ■ France

An attractive vanilla aroma and luscious fruit flavour with a hint of desiccated coconut combine to make this my favourite sweetie. Just right with game soup, pâté, foie gras or soft blue cheese like Roquefort.

DRY SPARKLING WHITE

Great Western Brut Reserve, Seppelt

■ £4.99 ■ Australia

Nicely rounded sherbet-like fizz with unaggressive dryness and a rich, vanilla-like flavour. Either drink as a great aperitif, or try it with a fruit-based pudding.

SWEET SPARKLING WHITE

Moscato d'Asti, Michele Chiarlo, 1992

■ £4.75 ■ Italy

Stylish honeyed fizz with lots of grapey flavours and a pleasant, zippy finish. Good with chocolate pudding.

DRY ROSE

Syrah Rosé, Vin de Pays d'Oc, Domaine des Fontaines, 1992

■ £2.95 ■ France

Made in a village which used to be the last staging post for thirsty mountain-going travellers in the 13th century, it's apt that this aromatic wine, with flavours of parma violet sweets and soft red fruits, is so gulpable.

INDEX

Page numbers with * denote Star Buys